LADY LEO

A STORY THAT MUST BE REPEATED

Poverty is not natural, it is created by humans and can be overcome and eradicated through the actions of human beings. And eradicating poverty is not an act of charity, it is an act of JUSTICE.
Mandela

Edgar Peña

Published by Ibukku, LLC
www.ibukku.com
Graphic Design: Diana Patricia González J.
Cover Design: Ángel Flores Guerra B.
Copyright © 2023 Edgar Peña
ISBN Paperback: 978-1-68574-502-8
ISBN Hardcover: 978-1-68574-504-2
ISBN eBook: 978-1-68574-503-5

Acknowledgements

The achievement of being able to tell this story, worthy of being told and immortalized as a family legacy, would not have been possible without the strongest feelings of love, gratitude, and admiration for my mother.

Making "Doña Leo" tangible had the collaboration of accomplices and allies... Thanks to Mónica Vargas, Special Educator who, hearing the story firsthand and believing in the value of the work, as well as the advice of journalist Madit Cabrera who, with zeal and professionalism, shaped this narrative. Together with her husband Rafael Pérez, they supported my creative process, always emphasizing that I am not a writer, but someone convinced that success stories, stories of overcoming obstacles, and of this high caliber of female empowerment are a mandatory task for future generations.

Prologue

This work is an expression of the author's joy who, without being a writer, was moved by the primal desire to convey to the reader the steps we must take in this earthly life, and even more, the lasting footprints that a magnificent woman left in her path through life: My beloved mother "Doña Leo".

Words fall short to describe everything that a mother's love can achieve, a mother of 8 children, being the backbone of a household. This life story takes place in the rural Colombia of a combative era, where gender stereotypes were even more pronounced, where there was a civil war, where control was disputed between two politically opposed poles, where insurgency was brewing in the countryside, and above all, where a woman, being a peasant, without the support of a family to embrace her and due to the twists of fate, managed to navigate all these adverse factors and rise above them, especially from a young age.

"Doña Leo", a peasant overshadowed by the misfortunes and humiliations of her time's society, with a heart eager for dreams and immense love for her children, is the genuine example of a mother's love, determination, and empowerment of a woman. For that era, it was unusual to see her in a role side by side with men, navigating myriad situations in the business world while firmly juggling her role as a mother.

With the Almighty as her guard and light, and love as her driving force to take on rugged and challenging paths, paths that led this brave woman to reap the rewards of her efforts, in the endless victory of a woman who, against all odds, adorned herself with personal and family successes. May this work serve as a testimony to inspire women and those who battle adversities every day but have a clear direction in cherishing and uplifting their most precious treasure, their family.

Chapter I

Amidst the remote landscapes of rural Colombia is where Leovigilda comes into life, in the municipality of Maripi, on September 3, 1925. For the remainder of this story, a story worthy of admiration and tribute, she will be simply "Leo".

This girl, who over the years would be known as "Doña Leo", spent her early years on a large farm in a warm climate, along with her family comprised of her father Gregorio Peña, her mother María Monroy, and 4 siblings: Adán, Celina, Jesus, and Leonilde, with Leo being the youngest of them all.

The farm, both beautiful and vast, was the dreamt-of and cherished home, forged from a beautiful love story between Leo's parents. It stands unforgettable for its pleasant spaces as much as the moments lived there. Broad and cozy corridors, spacious bedrooms distributed into two for the men and two for the women, and, of course, a much larger room designated for their parents. There was also a magnificent kitchen, where succulent aromas and flavors converged for the family's delight. Mrs. María, Leo's mother, dedicated and loving, centered her life in the kitchen, turning it into a gathering place for the family, where by the warmth of the stove, she could prepare regional dishes such as arepas, stuffed ripe plantains, and tamales. This commendable household task was accompanied by her sharing beautiful stories and interesting anecdotes with her children, tales from the 30 years of union that Gregorio and María proudly held.

The story of María and Gregorio dates back to the time when his family decided to move near the village; they were Spanish immigrants. One January afternoon, María's father, Carlos, told his wife, Julia, that he had met a pleasant man who offered to invest in honey production. Little by little, the families began to form a close bond, but the children María and Gregorio did not meet until years later by chance. The now young Gregorio, in search of a nearby farm, ran into María and decided to ask her for directions to the Jamaica estate... The attraction was immediate.

María and Gregorio were just teenagers when they felt the spark that would intertwine their lives for a long time. They merged their destinies in a marriage with solid foundations and eyes set on creating a family. Time gifted them moments of happiness with the arrival of their children. One by one, members were added to the household, to the big house; and Leo was the latest newborn to cross the doors of the estate, filling her father Gregorio's heart and eyes with light.

Leo was always considered the most blessed child among her siblings. Her natural beauty stood out when they styled her brown hair in a particular way on her head. Those who saw her said she looked as if she wore a golden crown. She was the perfect child, always the most helpful and attached to her father.

From a very young age, she felt the desire to work and learn about the tasks of the field, and unlike most girls her age, she would accompany Gregorio almost daily to work on the two farms he owned: the one in Maripí, where they all lived in warm lands with a sweltering temperature ranging between 36 and 38 degrees, where they produced honey and sugarcane; and the farm in colder lands, where they usually obtained milk and derived products that were sent to Maripí.

The Peñas Monroy planted almost everything they consumed: chili peppers, cilantro, plantains, coffee, cocoa, sugarcane... In short, everything that this generous land offered; but always with effort and love for what they did.

Between one farm and the other, there was a long path. On foot, it took eight to nine hours to get from one to the other, but the effort was rewarded by the view, filled with imposing landscapes that fascinated Leo. Accompanied by her father, she began to make these long trips daily to bring sustenance to her family. In a short time, she learned to ride the oxen and donkeys with Gregorio's help, and to drive the animals from one farm to the other with the canteens of water and milk, which would end up in the hands of her siblings and her mother.

Gregorio always taught his little daughter the "secrets of a good farmer" when harvesting the crops. Leo was fascinated by pulling the yucca plants out of the ground with her small hands; with a huge smile, she would watch how at the end of the stems, the large and tasty edible roots would appear. Of all the activities she learned from her loving father, this was the one she liked the most and the one she missed the most when, years later, she remembered her days as a farm worker.

In a short time, Leo, despite her young age, knew a lot about planting in the field, herding beasts, and how both farms were managed. She came to know the entire rural area with its beautiful country landscapes as the back of her hand; she never got lost among the many dirt roads that outlined the place. Every day, as she made the journey to the colder land with her father, they would see a modest school on the side of the road. Gregorio, always thinking about how bright his favorite daughter's future would be, knew that with her field knowledge and a good education, Leo would lack nothing in life. All doors would open, and knowledge would fall at her feet. That's why, every time they passed by the little house, he told the young girl that she should start her studies when she turned seven, but she never felt curious to do so.

Gregorio Peña was a very hardworking man. His parents, who came from Spain, taught him from a young age the value of work and the immense importance in life of having a well-established family and a home full of love and understanding, where values were the pillars that upheld the integrity of each member and inhabitant of the household. This is how this child became a fine young man, reaping the sweet benefits the area offered, cultivating honey, sugarcane, and panela. This unparalleled young man then became a good, honorable, hardworking, and impeccable man.

Gregorio turned this toil into the sustenance for his family, which kept growing in size and love after his marriage to María. Gregorio, mastering the arts of the land, from sunrise to sunset, labored diligently to bring bread to his home. Amidst such happiness and prosperity, misfortune struck, and the inevitable death came to Gregorio due to a prostate condition, which prematurely took him away from his beloved family at the age of 50.

Gregorio's departure was a sharp and hard blow to the family. Desolation and despair now reigned in that home. María suffered in silence, as if she had undergone the amputation of a part of her body; the pain was immense. The same went for their children who loved and revered their father. They remained like the morichales seen in the distance on the plains, swaying eternally in the breeze, especially Leo, who lost a companion, an accomplice, a mentor, her guide, her shield, her hope, her warmth on cold days, and a sprinkle of rain on hot days. Leo lost her compass, her teacher, the tender and protective hand she held every day on the endless dirt roads... Leo lost her father!

Not long after Gregorio's premature death, Jesús, one of Leo's older brothers, fell ill with leprosy. Jesús' life was reduced to the four walls of a room in a leprosarium. Little by little, he deteriorated like a dry leaf on a tree. In this way, he spent entire days watching the hours pass by through the window of his room. The sun rose, the stars came out, memories surfaced, anguish set in, hour after hour, minute by minute, until his body lost all its life force and stopped beating in this world.

The departure of Jesús affected María much more, who still couldn't wake up from the nightmare that meant opening her eyes every morning and remembering that Gregorio was no longer part of that duo that melted in love, and who shared the same air to live.

To cope with the absence, María kept herself busy with household chores. She learned to cry silently for the departure of her husband, knowing that the best tribute she could give to her husband's memory was to move her family forward.

To keep the family economy afloat, María raised animals, and for this, she relied on the help of her older children, who were responsible for feeding and caring for these animals. At noon, everyone would put on their work clothes and for long hours they would attend to all the needs that a pen required... However, "be careful not to neglect your school duties... You have to do house chores and school homework," María would tell them every day with a firm voice but with a loving tone.

In solitude, María had developed a system of habits that helped both clear her mind and feed her children, or even earn a little more money to invest in the family's well-being. In the mornings, at the break of dawn, she would walk silently to the pen where the cows were and begin her milking routine with great patience. Her thoughts would dissolve in the white foam that appeared on the surface of the milk as she hummed a song her mother had taught her in what now seemed like a very distant past. By the time the family members woke up for breakfast, they would find on the table large glasses of warm milk, always accompanied by arepas and corn rolls. The leftover milk María would set aside for sale or prepare delicious cheeses and butter, which were the delights of those who shared the table every morning.

The days went by, between monotony and a desire to forget, between inventing new ways to make money and walking through labyrinths of memories in love with the past. Moons and suns, droughts, and rainwater settled on the roof of the big house, bringing with them the law of life, the natural law of families where every member born within dreams of independence and grafting a new branch onto the family tree trunk. Over time, the core group of five slowly began to dissolve like salt in water, as several of the siblings went their separate ways.

Celina moved to Bogotá, the capital city of Colombia, to start a new life in the city. Fate granted her some happiness when she married a businessman named Manuel who made tires, and she had the calm and serene life she always longed for, the life she dreamt of on those steamy nights back in the hot lands. It's not that Celina didn't appreciate her family or love the land that gave her so much as she grew up, she simply "wanted more for her life." She wanted to see the world, see cities, have comforts, and of course, a man who loved her and gave her a family of her own.

Back at the hacienda, Leonilde remained. As she grew and matured as a woman, she maintained a passionate love relationship with a young man from the village, a relationship that brought two children into this world: Miguel and Joaquín... Time continued its course.

One day, Celina reached out to her sister Leonilde. She planted a seed in her mind, which would soon germinate with the idea that "there was no future in that village," that it would be better if she packed her bags and headed to Bogotá as soon as possible. According to Celina, there she would have a better quality of life and more job opportunities, and later on, she could bring her children and offer them a better future.

It wasn't long before Leonilde confronted María, her mother, with a candid conversation: she announced that she would follow in the footsteps of her sister Celina and would leave the children, aged four and two, under her care, with the help of Leo, who was the only girl left on the hacienda. After a short while, Leonilde set out on her new path; she took the few things she owned, packed them in a suitcase, and headed towards Bogotá, the road to a brighter future and a better tomorrow.

While in Bogotá, Leonilde lived with her sister Celina for a few months, who advised her that the best thing that could happen in her life was not to return to the village. As if a premonition, Celina's recommendation impacted Leonilde's fate... Two long years passed and Leonilde did not return to the village... and she would never do so again.

The tragic, unconfirmed story of Leonilde's death speaks of a rib fracture caused by a fight with her romantic partner. Yes, Leonilde found a companion in Bogotá, someone to watch the sunsets with and share the house they rented, share the table they bought, and dream in the bed they acquired. Unfortunately, not everything was rosy... Over time, the true character of that wonderful man came to light: a hidden violence, a sneaky bad temper emerged from the depths of that being.

Neighbors say that on a fateful day, the couple's usual argument could be heard from their home. Until a dull thud silenced everything... a blow that broke one of Leonilde's ribs, which resulted in a puncture in a lung, leaving her breathless forever.

The two children were left orphans in Maripí. They were left without a mother, but not alone; they were now under the protective wings of the guardian angels that Mrs. María and Leo represented.

Adán, the only man remaining in the family still residing in the big house, also felt life's call, and from his soul arose the need to have a companion by his side. Someone to feel the comforting embrace from after a full day of work, someone to spend the rest of his days with. He set out on his path and moved to a farm in the cold lands with a woman fifteen years older than him. The age gap was not a hindrance to finding happiness and finding peace in the essence of his woman.

In Maripí, when Leo found herself alone with her mother and the two children, she decided to abandon the studies she had started a few months earlier in honor of her father. But at just seven years old, she made the decision to lock away in her memory her brief time at the humble school she attended... a school with only two classrooms.

She and her mother spent some time working and surviving with the two children under their care. Leo, who already had experience in fieldwork despite her young age, developed a new sense, essential for her journey the rest of her life. She learned that by saving during sunny days, one can safely navigate through the storms of austerity.

The work done with her small hands yielded few fruits. She cleverly divided the amount earned: half went to meet the needs of the house, her mother, and her nephews; the other half of coins and bills ended up inside the mattress she used to sleep on and dream at night. This fact made her experience a feeling she wasn't familiar with, being so young. However, as time passed and she remembered those days, Leo realized what she felt was both pride and peace at the same time. She knew that someday that money would be used in a time of need, and no one in the house would lack anything.

On her part, locked in her room at night, wrapped in tears of loneliness, Mrs. María knew she was losing the battles of memories that reminded her daily that her husband, Gregorio, had joined the Creator years earlier. The pieces of her heart, shattered by the departure of her beloved, never wished to come together again. She knew she had to carry on for Leo and the children, but there was no longer a vital spark, there wasn't a star left for her to follow... She couldn't go on... and a few months later, she died.

Leo, at almost ten years old, was left alone with two children, aged six and four, to care for. She drew on the advice, practice, and skills her father had taught her and began to work on her own. She walked immense distances to Simijaca. The small feet of this girl left their mark on the many kilometers of paths that separated her from the fieldwork.

One fine day, Leo decided to offer food to some workers who were cultivating the field, and little by little, by cooking and selling that food, she managed to gather a bit more money.

This girl always stood tall and kept working. Her young mind had no time to get sidetracked by the usual distractions of a child just starting out on life's journey. Her main focus was always to live... If she lived, the children under her care would too.

Miguelito, the older boy, helped her with the food deliveries. They walked endless hours to reach each destination, and while all this was happening, Joaquín had to stay alone at home. This little one suffered from asthma and had to content himself withstanding daily at the doorway of the big house, watching as Leo and Miguel walked away on the paths, watching as their silhouettes grew smaller with the passing of minutes and distances. He knew it, his lungs told him: those journeys were very hard for him. Even though the climate was tropical mountainous, the fatigue affected him greatly.

Eight months passed before the shadow of death knocked again on the doors of the country house in the warm lands. Joaquín began to deteriorate, and the nearest health center was a five-hour walk away. Leo and Miguelito had no other choice but to prepare "aguitas" and home remedies, but they could not achieve their aim: Joaquín exhaled his last, anguished breath. He passed away from what seemed to be pneumonia.

The universe of people around Leo and Miguelito shrank even further. With the passage of clock hands and calendar pages, these children grew up and leaned on each other. They continued working from very early hours until well after the sun had set. By saving at every moment, they managed to buy pack animals for work and purchased oranges, potatoes, and other fruits, transporting them from one place to another. The work remained hard, the routes remained long, but looking back... never.

Leo was always admired by her neighbors for taking care of her nephew even when she was very young in age. By the age of fifteen, the long walks and the efforts typical of fieldwork had quickly transformed her body into that of a slender and striking woman with stunning beauty. As expected, the men of the village began to surround her, flatter her, and court her. But she, with a deep understanding of what life entails, was able to run an entire farm without allowing any abuse or taking advantage of men.

Despite the small age difference, just four years, Miguelito became like a son to her. Circumstances made them mature. They learned to rely on each other, and life lessons gave them tenacity and strength to become hardworking individuals.

With the passage of many workday dawns and restful evenings, Leo, with her great maturity, began to understand that the little family she had left, even if they were far away and only acted like ghosts that once inhabited the corridors of her life, could return from the oblivion they themselves sought, just to claim a part of her beloved farm.

Chapter II

With the inexorable passage of time, Leo and Miguelito continued their life's journey, where Leo, still a teenager, already foresaw her potential as a merchant. Every Sunday, she ventured into the Maripi market, where, alongside Miguelito, with the harvest from the Hoyo Caicedo farm, they ground sugar cane, produced honey and panela (unrefined whole cane sugar), and also began to resell products like oranges, bananas, fruits, and vegetables to continue earning their livelihood.

The year was 1941, where progress was rapidly blooming, and thus modernity in the area. In the village, they began the groundwork for the road, which immediately attracted an influx of trucks for transport. Leo, with her broad vision for business, saw a window of opportunity. Every Sunday, she would buy a larger amount of goods in Maripi to take them to Simijaca on Mondays and to Chiquinquirá on Wednesdays. Chiquinquirá, being a larger city, saw her sales increase substantially, and it became the starting point for her to fervently climb the ladder in her life as a merchant.

At almost 16 years old, Leo was a well-known merchant in the countryside. Her young age was a testament to her vigor and she inspired a lot of trust among the residents. With determination and persistence, she managed to save money and open an account at the state bank known as "Caja Agraria." Saving became a life principle for Leo, turning her into a conservative manager who only spent on the essentials in her day-to-day life with Miguelito.

The year 1941 continued when her sister Celina, who was still living in Bogotá, and her brother, Adán, decided to inform Leo that they had made the painful but practical decision to sell the warm-land farm and that they would split the money equally. The farm was sold a few weeks after the announcement. It was to be expected, as Leo and Miguelito had taken care of maintaining both the main house and the entire land in impeccable condition. She felt that by keeping it that way, beautiful and neat, more than just a pleasant and comfortable place to live, it was a tribute to her beloved father. This fact helped it sell at a very good price.

Leo and Miguelito would not be left out in the cold, homeless. Her brother Adán, who lived on the family's other farm, the cold-land one, had decided to move with his partner to a nearby area. Knowing that this would be their new home, Leo didn't waste time and, together with Miguelito, began to prepare for the move as soon as possible. They were lucky that the buyers of the main house allowed them a little time. So, within a month, Leo and Miguelito set off for the cold land. Every so often, she would turn her head and, over her shoulder, see the childhood home getting further and further away: the land she learned to work on with her father, the afternoons playing with her siblings, her mother's smoky kitchen. Leo felt a knot in her stomach, a tear choking her, leaving her breathless. Miguelito noticed what was happening. He took her hand, squeezing it tightly, letting Leo know that everything would be alright, that the future was ahead.

Leo was very accustomed to her merchant life in that town. She was very happy and at peace, but she wouldn't let the change of area set back everything she had achieved in the warm lands; on the contrary, she was pleased because she would have more money thanks to her inheritance. She could indulge herself and her nephew with occasional luxuries: they could buy quality clothing and shoes, or if they preferred, they could enjoy a delicious treat available in the area. The sense of savings that Leo had acquired over time made her realize that the inheritance money should be deposited in the bank for better use in the future, so she wouldn't squander it all at once.

That girl, who grew up under the care and teachings of her father and moved through life only with the company of a child who came under her care at a very young age, became an empowered and highly respected merchant in all the towns in the area.

It was only a matter of time before a young and beautiful peasant woman—hardworking, well-dressed, polite, respectful, and pleasant—would start to catch the suggestive glances of men. Suitors, compliments, flirtations, and attentions were everywhere for her.

Leo was unfamiliar with love; whispers of this feeling had never reached her ears, let alone carnal passions. Feeling praised and courted, little by little, she began to acknowledge the attentions from men, eventually finding herself attracted to the opposite sex, but she did not cross the threshold into the realm of the romantic.

But this wouldn't be the case forever. On a beautiful afternoon, quite casually, Leo experienced one of those rare moments that mark a lifetime: while shopping at the market of a nearby town, a piercing gaze met hers.

It was quicker than lightning…, it was a bullet shot from a gaze that pierced her chest, leaving her breathless. It was the gaze of Flaminio, a handsome young man who, in the company of his mother, quickly felt the embarrassment of the moment. And there, the brief yet intense moment ended.

Unknowingly, Leo spent hours thinking about the pleasant young man she had seen for just a few seconds. She simply couldn't get him out of her head for the rest of the day; she thought about how well-dressed he was, his beautiful dark hair, what his likes might be, and if he was thinking about her at that very moment.

Flaminio's parents, Mrs. Elena and Mr. Juan, had a family business by the roadside. "El Corte de la Ternera" was a restaurant where the specialty was grilled meat, although they also offered roast chicken and pork, all accompanied by exquisite arepas and salad, and if the customer preferred, any type of liquor.

Flaminio was the eldest son, the favorite of the Forero couple. He was a handsome young man, a good son, and an even better student. He attended classes at the student center located in Chiquinquirá, where his teachers had only praises for him due to his exemplary grades and excellent behavior.

Due to the distance that separated Flaminio from his family, the young man eagerly counted the days until he could reunite with his parents again. In the evenings, after intense study sessions and assignments, Flaminio would lay in his bed, longing for the weekend, when he would travel to the family farm in Maripí. Sometimes, he would visit the family business to see how he could help or just to feel close to his loved ones, even if there wasn't much to do.

The fate of Leo and Flaminio began to intertwine one Sunday morning when Leo walked into El Corte de la Ternera, offering products from the market to the restaurant. On that occasion, the visit proved unfruitful, as Mr. Juan explained that he was not interested in what Leo was offering at the moment and asked her to return the following week. Disappointed, she looked for the exit. As she crossed the door, a strong collision jolted her from her thoughts. She had come face to face with someone who, without hesitation, acted on his reflexes and grabbed her arm to prevent her from falling. As Leo regained her balance, she found herself looking straight into the eyes that had pierced her heart with a profound gaze: they were Flaminio's eyes. Leo's cheeks blushed fiery red once more. He, looking comfortable and radiating immense confidence, greeted her kindly and inquired what she was doing in his parents' restaurant. "My parents' restaurant," echoed inside Leo's head. She found it incredible that, out of all the places in the area, she had walked into that very one, the place where her captivating young man had walked its corridors countless times.

Swallowing hard, she dug deep within herself for the strength to explain, without showing any trace of nervousness, the reason for her visit to the restaurant. Flaminio, with insistence, assured her that she would have better luck the following week, as the restaurant would need to restock food. With nothing more to say, they both said goodbye.

From that goodbye, the week Leo spent waiting to see Flaminio again was pure torture. There were days when she watched the sun set and rise without closing her eyes for more than twenty minutes. It wasn't so much that she thought about that young man, but what his gaze and his presence made her feel. She spent sleepless nights thinking about how she would dress for that upcoming meeting, what she would say, how she would behave. It was a week where lethargy reigned for Leo, where she levitated on white clouds of a clear sky. With the impulsiveness of a wild gust of wind, Leo prepared for "the grand meeting" and used all her trading skills to coordinate with fruit and vegetable suppliers to reserve the finest produce for her meeting with Flaminio: "It had to be perfect, nothing could go wrong."

The big day arrived!

It couldn't be said that Leo woke up early, because in reality, she never managed to fall asleep. The chirping of crickets and the songs of nighttime frogs managed to lull her for moments, but the anxiety of seeing herself reflected in Flaminio's gaze once again kept her from sleeping.

She put on her best work clothes, styled her hair, took one last look in the mirror, and headed towards the Forero family's business, intent on selling the best products she had secured from the market. Truly, whether they bought the fruits and vegetables that day mattered little to her; she had other hopes. She wasn't too concerned when Mrs. Elena bought only a few items. Like the refined woman she was, Leo thanked her for the purchase, pivoted on her heels, and walked away, lamenting her double stroke of bad luck: she hadn't sold everything and hadn't seen... But there he was, Flaminio, with his broad smile and piercing gaze, making her forget it all. Without giving her a moment to catch her breath, he immediately and gallantly invited her, in front of his mother, to have a soft drink at a nearby place.

Leo felt like she was floating; her feet weren't touching the ground. As she walked alongside Flaminio, there were moments when she wanted to grasp his hand. Not to claim him or show him off to everyone they passed, but rather to ground herself, lest she rise up and drift away like an untethered fairground balloon.

They talked for hours, sharing laughter and getting to know each other better. They made plans to meet again in the coming days, after Flaminio returned from Chiquinquirá, where he was studying. Meanwhile, Leo continued working to support herself. Despite being close in age, their life circumstances were starkly different.

Once again, Leo's nights stretched on endlessly. However, every moment of lost sleep was justified each time she reunited with Flaminio. Their encounters became a frequent occurrence as the months went by in Maripí. With every meeting, Leo's feelings grew stronger, and Flaminio became increasingly attentive and affectionate. Gradually, they started a relationship. Even though they couldn't see each other as often as most young couples in love, due to Flaminio's recurring trips to his school, their bond only solidified.

As time passed, they became more and more intertwined. Leo felt a rising passion within her. Even without any prior experience in the realm of physical desire, her body yearned to surrender to its call, much like a leaf that falls into a river, drifting along its gentle waters, being pulled by eddies and swift currents, until finally reaching the blissful safety of the shore.

Without any prior planning, one sultry evening, at the tender age of nineteen, Leo allowed Flaminio to leave an indelible mark on her life. Their perspiration mixed, creating an intense bond. That night, Leo transitioned from girlhood to womanhood. Flaminio was the one; he would forever be etched in her memory as the man who introduced her to the realms of physical passion. And so it was.

During one of those intimate encounters, where love was at its peak, laid out on the grass of a neighboring field, Flaminio confessed something to Leo that no woman ever wants to hear: "My parents don't agree with this," a statement that clouded Leo's peace. "They think it will distract me from my studies and the life plan they've set out for me." After a pause, Flaminio told Leo that he didn't care about his parents' opinions; after all, it was his life, and he wanted to continue seeing her, though covertly.

Even though Flaminio tried to calm Leo and reassure her, his words were not entirely truthful. In fact, they were a half-truth. The raw reality was that Flaminio's parents had sternly warned him to end the relationship, and if he continued to see her, they would not allow him to return to the village. For his parents, Flaminio was the son who would inherit the family legacy; all their hopes for the family business rested on him. They envisioned him as an upstanding man, a pillar of a respectable family, and not with a peasant girl who had no family, no education, who worked as a trader to support herself and a child who was not even her own.

But this hidden truth didn't stay in the shadows for long. On a fateful day for Leo, she came face-to-face with Mr. Juan, Flaminio's father. He cruelly told her that she wasn't worthy of a man like Flaminio, a prosperous young man who deserved a decent woman from a good family.

Leo was devastated, with a lingering wound in the recesses of her mind.

Leo kept pushing forward with the relationship. The young woman never missed an opportunity for a clandestine meeting with Flaminio, who, at first, presented himself as a thoroughly responsible and enamored man. However, as time passed, it became evident that the daily words spoken by his parents began to chip away at the conscience of the twenty-year-old boy.

Leo still felt butterflies in her stomach every time she saw her young lover approaching. Every day she felt more in love and had the strength to keep fighting for their future. Flaminio, on the other hand, began to take things more lightly. Over time, he realized he had never been prepared for a full commitment to Leo. Influenced by his parents, he began to see their relationship more as an adventure and a rebellion typical of his age.

After a few passionate months, Leo, while walking through the market, felt an unusual fatigue. Everything around her seemed to spin, she felt weak and out of place. It was at that moment a thought struck her like a bolt of lightning; the world froze, and with eyes as wide as saucers, she realized her menstrual cycle hadn't come. It was delayed or perhaps it wouldn't come for quite a long time. She placed her hands on her belly and knew instantly, without a doubt: inside her was growing the fruit of her first love, her only love, her first man, her only man: Flaminio.

Sadly, this revelation hit Leo on one of the days when Flaminio was away from the village. Once again, she found herself alone, faced with days filled with anxiety and loneliness, enduring endless sleepless nights.

Nervously and anxiously, she waited for the slow passing of the days to reunite with her beloved and tell him what was happening inside her womb, inside her life. But she had to wait even longer with that news lodged in her throat because, on the usual day of Flaminio's arrival, he did not show up.

One more week felt like twenty years in Leo's mind. Every day she went to the path where Flaminio used to arrive, hoping that perhaps he would appear and tell her, "My classes got complicated. I've arrived now, here I am for you," but this never happened.

In her mind, Leo imagined the different reactions her beloved could have upon learning the news of his impending fatherhood: Would he be happy? Would he be upset? Would they embrace tightly, or would he simply turn around and leave? But she never imagined, not even for a second, the avalanche that was about to hit her. When Flaminio finally appeared in the village, she, without any preamble, opened the floodgates of her mouth and let out the news that drenched the young student like a cascade of cold water:

"I'm pregnant."

Leo was left stunned by Flaminio's reaction, who with just three questions tore her entire life apart in a mere second:

"Do you know who the father is? How many other men have you been with? Are you making up this story to tie me down and marry me, a good family man?"

Leo felt in every cell of her body something she didn't quite understand. A mix of anger, profound sadness, and astonishment flooded her body and soul, until she realized she had never in her life felt so offended. Thus, in a matter of seconds, she decided to turn around and leave Flaminio standing there with his arrogance... She never wanted to see him again.

The feeling that overcame Leo when Flaminio insulted her could have lasted a month, a year, a decade. However, knowing that soon she would have another mouth to feed, she decided to go to Doña Elena and Don Juan's restaurant to talk to their son and ask him to take some responsibility in this whole matter. A week after the unpleasant incident, Leo showed up at the door of "El Corte de la Ternera." Immediately, the Forero couple blocked her way, only to deny her entry to the establishment and tell her that Flaminio had left the village and would not return for a long time... a time that turned into forever. Flaminio never came back.

Leo set aside her characteristic toughness and allowed herself to cry. She let the paths leading to the farm get flooded with her tears, and the mattress where she tried to sleep and the pillow she rested her head on melted like cotton candy when it touches water. Leo let the farm animals see her cry, she let the Moriche palms see her cry. Sometimes she would stop just to wonder where the tears came from in her body, how they didn't dry up, only to start crying again. She felt that the rivers swelled with her tears, that the tides would sweep away entire coastlines because of her tears.

Leo allowed herself to spend entire days without strength, lying in bed with her arms outstretched as if nailed to a cross. In the end, Flaminio turned out not to be the one. She couldn't believe that her beloved prince had treated her that way.

The first to taste her flesh, the first to whom she gave herself entirely, the first with whom she thought she'd spend the rest of her days... The first to plant a seed of life within her. There was nothing left to do but mourn him to exhaustion, until he was forgotten.

The young girl decided to distance herself from everything, rarely leaving the cold land estate. She was accompanied by Miguelito, the boy who was always her strongest support, who would never let her down, who had become her greatest ally, her biggest support.

Leo would face her pregnancy knowing that she wouldn't have the same freedom of movement nor the same ease to work. She knew that life would change drastically for her, a change from heaven to earth, a turn with no going back. There were times when she thought that a little child might become a burden, but she immediately shook her head vigorously from side to side as if trying to erase such a terrible thought about an innocent being who hadn't even come into this world yet. Holding onto her maturity and strength, she knew she could handle the situation in the best way possible, knowing that now she'd have to work less but earn more money. A solution had to be found, a strategy needed to be devised.

Even though she didn't want to, even though it might have been better to erase him from her memory forever, she knew that the best support she could have in raising her child would come from its father. For months, she tried to find the child's father, but it was in vain. Flaminio had disappeared from the map of her life, as if the earth had swallowed him whole. Yet, Leo knew it had been his parents who had influenced the young man to never show his face again. In an honorable family, it was frowned upon for their son, a highly respected student, to have romantic liaisons, and even more so to impregnate an orphaned girl.

It was pouring rain when Leo asked Miguelito to go to the neighboring farm and bring back Mrs. Petra. The pains below her belly had come without warning. She stood by the window, watching the rain fall when she felt a liquid run down her inner thighs, reaching her ankles. The time had come; there was no turning back now. A new child would come into the world that very night.

Mrs. Petra entered the house drenched from the rain. Had it not been raining, drops of sweat would've appeared on her forehead from the effort of the run she had to make, urged by the news that Miguelito had brought her. There was Leo, lying on the same bed where she had cried so much for the father of the child who would take its first breath of life today.

Alirio Peña, named after his mother Leo's last name, was born on the night of May 28, 1945. A night of storms, thunder, and lightning.

Leo felt as helpless as that child; she felt like both were newborns in this world. Both were shaking as they lay on the bed, Leo from fear and Alirio from cold. Leo thanked heaven for the timely attention of Mrs. Petra, who was no stranger to the task of bringing children into the world, as she was the local midwife. Glory be to God! Petra, neighbor, friend, and midwife, and now, Leo's teacher in the art of caring for a newborn child.

Once again, Leo took a leap forward on the timeline of life; with one jump, she climbed several steps on the path to adulthood, towards mature life. All of this was new, of course, nothing typical for her young age.

It was a tumultuous time for Leo. Love radically changed her life. The promise of life and future she found in the deep gaze of a handsome young man turned into a downward spiral of bitterness and loneliness.

Yes, she was alone with two children in her care: one just opening its eyes to the world, dependent on endless care, and another child who, despite his young age, became her faithful companion and pillar of support. However, he too couldn't fend for himself in a world where if you didn't work, you simply couldn't survive.

It was a tremendous crossroads for young Leo. She constantly thought about needing to work to put food on the table, but she had a child whom she couldn't leave without care. She didn't know what to do.

Leo's significant leaps in maturity brought with them a new layer to the armor that life was placing on her, piece by piece. She was now beginning to realize her new reality, how uphill everything would become at home, in her life... All of this, coupled with a massive first heartbreak that weighed on her, even if she didn't want to admit it, as heavy as a boulder over her head.

As time passed, the thought began to grow in her mind that no man would take her seriously because she was a single mother. It was a fear that her youth nourished day by day in her head. She always thought that being a beautiful and hardworking woman, she could find a good man, but that wasn't the case: the men she would meet later would come and go from her life. She was constantly abandoned, which led her to feel, unfortunately, like an object.

Later on, Leo would realize that she was often rejected for her strong character. Time and the blows that life had dealt her had turned her into a tough person. She tried not to let herself be manipulated by men and was not submissive; on the contrary, she was assertive and self-sufficient, and this was not well-received by men.

None of this deterred Leo, who with each stumble found a way to move forward.

Chapter III

Two months after Alirio's birth and edging close to her 20th year, we find Leo adjusting to her new life, fully embracing her role as a single mother, where her priority was the wellbeing of the baby and Miguelito. Faced with such responsibility, Leo's mind pondered how she could go out to work, to market as she had been doing, to move in her usual business dealings, and thus be able to provide food for her home, maintain the farm, and look after the wellbeing of the two children under her care. There was no time to mend her broken heart or dwell on her past... only to look with determination at her present and her future.

Leo quickly understood that her life had changed forever. Her trading activities would have to take a complete turn; everything would be very different from how she had been doing it, as her new responsibilities would not allow her to go to markets and visit towns in the way she had done before.

But income had to be generated. So, Leo gradually began to leave the house for short periods to sell only honey and some other products—everything, because of time constraints, in smaller quantities than she was used to... But something was better than nothing. Often, when she made the decision to leave the farm, she would leave Alirio under the care of Miguelito. She always did it for just a few hours, with the constant worry of having left a baby in the hands of a child.

On other occasions, she ventured out with both children to conduct her business, but it was not at all easy for her to move along those dusty roads, much less to make her purchases with such a fragile creature in her arms.

One day, during one of those wanderings, Leo saw a rental sign on a house located by the Maripí road. The place was called Buena Vista.

"What if I rent that house and set up a shop?" Leo's thought spread its wings.

The whole way back to the farm was a back-and-forth of ideas sprouting from her entrepreneurial roots. Always visionary. Always applying her father's advice. She thought it would be for the best: a house by the side of the road. She would sell her products without having to leave, and thus could take care of the children more easily. Besides, Miguelito was already twelve years old and could easily help her with this new venture.

Leo's hunch was mainly based on the location of that house, on the edge of a busy road, a route that connected one town to another and was heavily trafficked all the time. In the front part, she would set up the business, where everyone passing by would feel compelled to stop and, even if it were out of sheer curiosity, look at all the products Miguelito would offer them, while she supervised or took care of Alirio at that moment.

Upon arriving at the farm, after finishing the chores, Leo prepared to sleep, always with the idea of the new business in her head, an idea that grew more and more in her brain in just one night.

Time had taught Leo that things shouldn't be overthought. You have to follow your hunch, as they call it. Twenty years old, a baby in her arms, and a child under her care—there was nothing more to think about. As soon as the first rays of morning light appeared, Leo got ready and left the farm in search of the owners of that roadside house, her future business location, her convenience, and her new future.

It can't be denied that the owners of that house looked Leo up and down when she expressed her interest in renting it immediately. They were taken aback by the fact that a young woman of twenty, with two children in tow, would conduct herself that way in business. They were surprised that at such a young age she was such a mature and visionary individual. But Leo's name held weight in any job decision in the area. Her reputation as a merchant preceded her, and that's how, without much thought, that married couple, the owners of the house, handed her the keys to her future business.

There was little to take from the farm. Both Leo and Miguelito felt this change would be temporary... The farm, which legally became Leo's due to an agreement between siblings, would be their home forever, or at least that's what they held in their thoughts.

For a moment, Leo felt that she could at least ease her concerns about taking care of Alirio while she worked. She felt that, finally, after a few months of hustle and bustle, she could lie flat on her back in a bed, stretch her arms out like a cross, exhale all her anguish, and finally find a restful sleep, the kind she so desperately needed. For this reason, she didn't hesitate for a second about the name with which she would christen the house... "Mi refugio" (My refuge), Leo expressed, relieved as the little house began to appear in the distance on the horizon of the path, which both she and Alirio and

Miguelito were traveling at that moment with some boxes and bags containing the essentials for living, a small move for a big step into the future.

It took them just two days to equip the store. But Leo, with her experience behind her, decided that the store would not only sell fruits, vegetables, and greens; she thought of expanding the range and also offering sodas, beers, and more dry goods. With a lot of faith and hope, they painted eye-catching signs with the intention of attracting customers, and it worked: in a short time, the "Mi Refugio" store was on everyone's lips. The locals knew that by just heading there, they would find what they were looking for in terms of food, and they would always be greeted with the attention of the beautiful Leo, Miguelito's personalized service, and a smile from little Alirio.

A year went by. 356 days of hard, continuous work in the store, serving customers, getting to know new locals, and of course, establishing new contacts for their businesses. They went to the farm less often than they wanted, but they were convinced it was a sacrifice to establish and build credibility for the business. This period was a time to adapt to their new home, a term Leo used to describe the place where the three of them would forge their future.

But deep down, Leo felt that this wasn't enough. While sales in the store were going smoothly, she felt the need to venture again into the paths of commerce to achieve even more, to face stormy times with what's saved in the bank account. Yes, savings were always at the forefront of Leo's mind, and the store didn't offer much margin for money to be set aside.

It was time to entrust young Miguelito with even more responsibilities; it was time to leave him in charge of the store while she went out to seek and sell more merchandise beyond the safe walls of "Mi refugio". After all, Miguelito already knew most of the area's customers and would know how to behave in front of new ones. The business had already become a reference point among the locals and travelers.

Without further delay, on a Monday at six in the morning, Leo resumed her travels.

In previous days, she had held a long and serious conversation with Miguelito. They discussed his new responsibilities regarding the store and taking care of Alirio. Once again, Miguelito's maturity shone through, and taking her hands, looking deep into her eyes, he promised Leo that while she was away, everything would go well... He would look after both Alirio and the store, and she could go back to trading without any hitches.

For several months, Leo kept up with her travels. Even though she always kept Alirio and Miguelito in her thoughts, she felt free once again to do something useful for the well-being of her small family unit. With a hint of guilt, she acknowledged that she wasn't the kind of woman to stay at home; she needed to traverse the roads and work in what she loved most, commerce. Considering what it meant to care for a baby and a store simultaneously, Leo decided to travel only three times a week. This way, they all adjusted to this new routine.

Young José Martínez appeared in the store on a hot morning. By fate's design, Leo was at the counter of Mi Refugio that day. Miguelito had gone to rest for a bit. The average-height young man with green eyes walked through the door and immediately flashed a mischievous smile at Leo, characteristic of men who know what they want. Although he was a local, the truth is that Leo didn't recognize him from anywhere. He was a complete and mysterious stranger to her eyes.

With the excuse of buying anything in the store, José kept coming to the place just to see Leo. Although there wasn't an overt courtship on his part towards her, the fact that he visited the establishment daily hinted at some kind of interest in the young woman. Leo still felt the fresh wounds, skin deep, left by her relationship with Flaminio. She had built a strong fortress around herself, a structure so tall and sturdy that no man could climb or penetrate it; it was up to José to find a crack through which to enter her heart.

Although she initially kept him at a distance from her life, Leo and José eventually developed a lovely friendship. It was hard for her not to waver in the face of the gallantry and good treatment that this young man offered her daily.

For several months she continued her life, working and taking care of the children; she never left her store or her trips to the market, she always kept busy. She visited the farm more regularly to make sure everything was fine, but now there was a difference: she wasn't alone while Miguelito and Alirio were at the store; now José was always there, to lend her a hand when she needed it.

It took some time for Leo to let her guard down, but she did. She built bridges towards love, always cautiously, yet once again enchanted by the spell of enthusiasm, for life had given her a new presence to help her cope with daily life: a generous man, cooperative, very beloved in the town, although she didn't know it, a good person from a good family, who at that time lived with his parents in Hoyo Caicedo.

It wasn't long before José moved into "Mi refugio". Little by little, its inhabitants learned to live under the same roof. The new family member quickly adapted to work in the store and life in the house, which promised a peaceful coexistence.

Alongside José's aspirations, the family grew. When Leo realized she was pregnant, she took it in stride and the news was well-received by the rest of the household, especially for José. Despite his young age, he already knew he wanted to start a family, a family of his own with the young Leo.

And so it was that on October 8, 1947, Isaura was born, a beautiful girl born from the love between Leo and José... Leo's first daughter, José's first child.

This girl came to further strengthen the bonds of family life in "Mi Refugio." With Isaura's first cry within the house, everyone perfectly understood that a family nucleus had formed within those walls. The time had come to work even harder, together, as it should be.

At that time, children's surnames were formalized through baptism; and although Isaura never took her father's surname because she never went through a baptismal font, she was the apple of José's eye, the girl who had come into the world to light up her parents' lives and strengthen the couple's bond with a tender smile.

For their part, José's family stopped sending him money, not because they were against what their son did with his life, but because now, as head of the household, he had to find his own means of support while Leo carried out her motherly duties with their new little one... Thus, everyone threw themselves into the task of growing the store even more, especially

Miguelito, who by then was already fourteen years old, old enough to become a hardworking teenager, a crucial piece in the smooth running of the household.

After a few months, Leo, always active and in search of more income for her home, decided to resume her trips to the villages to sell merchandise and thus reconnect with old customers whom she had practically forgotten about because she was fully involved in her new life. She didn't know if she had already lost them, if her loyal buyers had found new suppliers; only visiting them would give her that answer. Only by leaving the house could she bring more financial stability to the home.

She understood this perfectly; her years of experience in business pushed her to go out, but José didn't see it that way. He felt that his wife should be at home by his side, with him, with their family, with their new daughter. "There will come a time when the store alone won't provide enough for us to eat," Leo kept telling José, who, after some time and still with annoyance, understood both the situation and the fact that he was living with a woman who by nature was not one to stand still waiting for money to come to the door of the business; she was the one who had to go out and find it.

Leo would leave very early and return a few hours later. Upon arriving, her life partner was always in the store waiting for a customer, a fact that increasingly took its toll on José's mind. He continued to express his discontent with the life they were leading and demanded that his wife stay home. However, with her strong character, she never understood him.

A few months after resuming her routine on the paths and markets of the area, Leo began to feel tired. Sleep overwhelmed her body throughout the day, and she only wanted to stay in bed. She thought she was falling ill, until she noticed the absence of her menstrual period. "It can't be!" Her astonishment paved the way to a new reality: she was pregnant again.

Blinded by the shock and, deep down, frustrated by the prospect of once again having to momentarily halt her work life, Leo came to think that this new pregnancy might have been something José had planned just to keep her at home. But she accepted her reality and remained active. She simply wasn't accustomed to being home all day. She was a woman who had grown up amidst markets and fields, so, despite her pregnancy, she worked until her body allowed her to.

On November 9, 1948, her second daughter, Margarita, was born. A beautiful girl who brought joy back to the household, but sadly, it wouldn't last for long.

After recovering from childbirth, Leo resumed her journeys along the paths leading to towns and markets. Despite José's disapproval, Leo continued her routine activities outside the house, which brought storm clouds under the roof of "Mi Refugio" (My Refuge), leading to arguments everywhere. The stereotypes of the time and the marked generational machismo weighed on José. He was a young man who had become the father of two girls and, coming from a loving and well-constituted family, he didn't think it was right for a woman to be on the town streets, mingling with male traders, while he was left in charge of the children and tending to the sales of the business. José's complaints and demands towards Leo were constant: she was now a mother and wife, she should change her lifestyle and become a homemaker. Leo never accepted that mindset; she continued her trips and her work as a merchant.

One evening, Leo returned home only to find José standing at the door with a suitcase by his side. That young man decided he wouldn't engage in another battle with the indomitable Leo. Surrendering to the weight of exhaustion and frustration due to his wife's rebellious and defiant attitude, José looked at her intently and, without uttering a word, from the million he might have wished to say at that moment, he grabbed his belongings, made his way past her, and returned to his parents' home, never to come back again.

Deep down, Leo knew she had brought this outcome upon herself, but her pride was greater than any abandonment; she was not willing to negotiate her independence with any man. Once again, her strong character prevailed at another stage of her life.

Alone. Again alone surrounded by children. With four in her care, Leo made the decision to close the store and return to the farm in the colder land. She no longer wanted to be in the house, which, although it had brought them many joys and had welcomed two girls from her womb, had also become a reminder that married life is difficult if the partners are not in perfect harmony.

Leo, her son Alirio, her girls Isaura and Margarita, and her always present and invaluable Miguelito, set out for the farm to start over. It seemed that this would be Leo's life: new beginnings over and over for the rest of her days... new beginnings without looking back, but beginnings and endings that left her with great experiences and deep scars.

It wouldn't be long before Leo received another heavy blow.

While in the colder lands, the now-teenage Miguelito began working in the fields as a day laborer. With this daily work, the young man brought some money home, but Leo, with her imposing character, demanded more help around the house and in the business, something he saw as unfair. With all the strength of rebellion typical of his age, he began to confront Leo more and more.

He always saw, perceived, and respected her as a mother, but he began to feel that Leo's treatment towards him was like that of a boss to her worker. Night after night, amid arguments, this feeling filled his soul with more pain and anger, until he reached the point of deciding to pack his belongings in a sack and escape through the window of his room without any direction, crossing the darkness of the night.

Leo was left alone with the children... again.

The loneliness and pain left behind by Flaminio and José were incomparable to that of Miguelito. One can find love along the way; company, assistance, a child, not so much. Once again, Leo found herself at the crossroads of uncertainty... Now without help or support.

As always, there was no time to cry, let alone stop. She needed to find a way to work to feed her children, and so she did... With three young ones in tow, Leo continued, though not as frequently, of course, to tread the paths that led her to the markets of nearby villages. Keep buying, keep selling... that was everything, there was nothing else.

Those were days of deep exhaustion, days when she thought about staying on the farm and doing nothing, releasing the fatigue from her legs, but she simply couldn't afford that luxury.

One afternoon the following month, someone knocked on Leo's door. Three knocks that would bring life back to her body. When she opened the door, there stood Adán, her older brother, in the doorway, and behind him was a young man with tired eyes: it was Miguelito. Adán had brought back her comrade in a thousand battles, the commander-in-chief in the wars of life.

What Miguelito did during his absence remains a mystery to this day. Adán said that he found him by chance on a street in a neighboring village. Miguelito explained that he had been living with his father, but given the state in which he was found, that story is questionable. The important thing is that the young man had returned, that he was well and willing to continue working as a part-time laborer and help more with the chores on the farm.

So the months passed, in healthy peace and harmony...

One day, Mr. Nersario, the owner of the neighboring farm, knocked on Leo's door. He greeted her very kindly and asked her to sit down for a conversation without saying much more. Leo, puzzled, prepared coffee and hurriedly placed a chair in front of the man.

"Has something happened?" Leo asked without further hesitation.

Nersario, an older, well-groomed gentleman, lived on the neighboring farm with his wife Clotilde and their two children. They had always maintained a rather distant relationship for neighbors, so Leo was puzzled by his visit.

The man very slowly took a breath.

"Mrs. Leo, my family and I want to buy your farm. We want to expand ours, and yours is ideal for us."

Leo was taken aback, her eyes wide open, drowning in a profound silence. When she finally managed to find her voice, all she could muster was:

"Give me a few days to think about it."

But deep down, she knew she wouldn't need many days. She knew herself, she knew that her decision, whether negative or positive, would be made quickly.

Always thinking about business and how to keep her family afloat, Leo saw Nersario's proposal as a way to invest, and therefore, an opportunity to improve her life. What briefly held her back was the thought of what to do if she sold the farm.

As she never made a wrong move in business, before giving an answer, she decided to visit some farms in the area that were for sale. She remembered that a few months ago she had seen one not too far away called El Cubo, a fairly large estate.

Leo slept that night with the image of the estate embedded in her dreams, which she took as a premonition. "I'm going to buy that land first thing tomorrow," she envisioned herself saying to her reflection in a mirror while floating inches above the bed. She woke up excited. There was no time to waste; she would go right after her round through the local markets.

Leo was traveling along a long dusty road when, in the distance, the entrance to the estate began to appear. Two white pillars held up a sign reading: "El Cubo."

At that moment, her heart was leaping inside her chest. It was an opportunity that, if realized, would take her life and that of her family to another level. She already felt like a true matriarch, implementing all she had learned from her father about the countryside. She saw herself on horseback, riding through the lands, herding cattle, feeding the animals... Ultimately, she envisioned herself as the owner of a land that would fill her with pride and stability, something never seen in a woman from the area.

Leo opened the gate of the hacienda and headed to the main house. Her doubt turned into anxiety: After dreaming so much, would the hacienda still be for sale? With every step, she loved more of what she saw: the grand house, the stables, a lake, palm groves... She knocked on the wooden door. Only a few seconds passed, which to Leo felt like years, and a woman opened it. It was Mrs. Cortez, the owner of the hacienda, along with her husband.

"I've come to discuss business," said Leo. "I love the hacienda, but I'll leave it to you, who have lived here for many years, to convince me to buy it."

The Cortez couple assured her that it would be the ideal place for her and her family. Leo left there with the utmost enthusiasm, ready to give her neighbors a positive response.

Only six days had passed since Mr. Nersario's visit... in just six days, Leo had decided to turn her life around with a step as significant as selling the farm to which she was tied by a bond of memory roots. But she thought further ahead, she saw it as a business. El Cubo was a hacienda where she could plant and have animals that would generate profit. This way, she could spend more time with her children to teach them about the chores of the countryside, just as her father had done with her.

Within a few days, Leo sold her farm, while simultaneously negotiating for El Cubo. She had to tread carefully, taking meticulous steps in the negotiations, since her new acquisition was larger and more comprehensive in services. She had to dip into her savings for the purchase. Always keeping in mind the money she had diligently saved in the Caja Agraria, she didn't think twice about investing it fully in the cattle ranch, a dairy farm with vast corridors, abundant water sources, pastures, and beautiful fields that produced plenty of grass. She felt very proud of the steps she had taken in her adolescence, which had led her to the realization of this dream: to own the largest hacienda in the region... to have the documents that stated it was hers and no one else's.

Leo had run out of money. She didn't have any to buy animals or start planting, but she was only days away from moving, immersed in a great dream, to her new home.

The business deal between the Cortez family and Leo took place over several sessions spanning multiple days. Transferring ownership of a property of such magnitude was no simple task; the documentation had to be crystal clear, leaving no room for error; the handing over and depositing of money also had to be perfectly transparent, accounting for every last cent before handing over the keys.

The day before the final closing of the deal, Mr. Mario Cortez attended the meeting accompanied by his nephew, Clemente Cortez. A handsome young man standing at 1.80 meters tall, with brown hair, well-educated, and impeccably dressed, he immediately set his eyes on Leo. He had already heard stories about her beauty and her confidence when it came to business. However, Clemente felt that everything he had been told about this woman fell short upon meeting her in person. His first, instinctual response was to praise Leo for purchasing such a beautiful hacienda. What truly captivated him about the young woman was this great achievement she had attained on her own, through her own means, with her own money, without having to depend on anyone else. It was love at first sight.

Clemente had to wait seven days to see Leo again. His sorrow intermittently turned to hope each time he remembered the face of that beautiful woman. Yes, he acknowledged daily that he had been smitten by the empowered countrywoman, the new mistress of El Cubo. The day came when Mr. Cortez arrived with his nephew for the final signing, the moment that would put the entire future into Leo's hands. A handshake and an intense exchange of glances between the young pair ensued.

Mr. Cortez made himself entirely available to Leo, a moment Clemente wouldn't waste to direct his entire arsenal of compliments and gallantry towards the new owner of the hacienda. To the surprise of all present, the charming young man freely expressed his desires and feelings, promising Leo that he would not leave her alone and would frequently visit her in a friendly manner.

It seemed that the flames of passion would reignite in Leo's soul. With two past disappointments, doubt towards men had started to grow within her. But fate took it upon itself to teach her that no adviser was worse than loneliness. She saw the possibility of feeling loved again, of being accompanied and supported, with the added thrill of having instantly captivated a man desired by many women in the town. A very attractive man who caught the attention of many for his demeanor, education, and respectable family background.

Leo and her family's relocation took place during a very tumultuous time for Colombia: tension grew between liberals and conservatives, escalating dramatically with the assassination of the candidate most likely to become the nation's president, Jorge Eliezer Gaitán. This event ignited widespread tension across the country.*

Leo witnessed the rise in violence, reaching depths where men displayed the basest of animal instincts. She saw the emergence of "Las Chusmas," irregular militant groups that, without any negotiation, would storm properties to cold-bloodedly murder those whose political beliefs did not align with theirs.

These were extremely harsh times that deeply scarred the lives of peasants. Often, out of fear of an unwelcome visit from Las Chusmas, they had to sleep in different locations and in groups.

Clemente quickly proved that he was a man of his word and fulfilled his promises. He assisted Leo with her move and frequently visited them. Leo was eternally grateful for this because, even though she considered herself a fiercely independent woman, the presence of a man was crucial during these times of political turmoil.

*(Translator Note: Jorge Eliezer Gaitán's assassination in 1948 is historically significant and is considered to have been one of the triggers for the period known as "El Bogotazo" and the subsequent era of violence in Colombia called "La Violencia." This was a time of significant political and social unrest, resulting in the deaths of many Colombians.)

As expected, Leo found herself gradually succumbing to the gallant young man's advances. Little by little, she fell in love.

She felt that with Clemente, she could build what she couldn't with José: both a romantic and a business relationship, a successful partnership. Since Clemente was intimately familiar with the world of farming, he would understand her far better than José had. They would have mutual support, paving the way for a future filled with love and stability.

The decision to let Clemente into her heart was made. He presented himself as the perfect man: supportive in love and finances, a man free from vices, without any apparent flaws, and always genuine and courteous.

Although José had exited Leo and her daughters' lives when she decided to return to colder lands, he didn't hide his irritation and disappointment when he found out there was a new man in the life of the woman he had loved so deeply. It's said that once, during a public gathering in the plaza, he expressed that he never wanted to see his daughters again. Seeing them would remind him of Leo's face, and that was a visage he wished to forever erase from his memory. Stories tell of José embarking on a journey to forget, wandering through various towns and cities. Some even claimed they received letters from him with letterheads from countries they didn't even know existed. José faded out of everyone's lives.

Unfortunately, over time Leo began to see with pain and concern how Clemente's true face was revealed behind a mask, which, as the days went by, was falling to pieces on the ground of disappointment. She couldn't understand why Clemente had done this to her and her family. Why did he charm them all with lies of love? The truth is he wasn't the man they hoped he would be.

Another disappointment was on the horizon, but Leo couldn't blame her major flaw of being swayed by the gallantries of handsome men who presented themselves as hard-working and trustworthy, whom, despite her strength, easily deceived her; no, what Clemente did was pure enchantment.

After presenting himself as an ideal man, Clemente showed that he liked liquor, getting drunk frequently at parties or places he went to alone. He didn't help at all on the estate and became a burden. He only sought to satisfy his sexual desires with Leo, even though his reputation as a womanizer was rapidly growing in the village, as he had always been a man desired by women.

As a result of these carnal encounters, Leo became pregnant again. Her fourth child, Eliseo, was born on October 26, 1951.

The fights at home increased along with the disappointments, and Miguelito decided not to witness the disintegration of his home again. He simply couldn't stand the situation anymore and chose to set out on the path of existence once again. He left alone under a roof of stars with life, just life, as his destination.

Once again, Leo found herself alone surrounded by people. Once more, she had to face the path of hard work in a desert of people. Her experiences with men felt like plowing the sea.

Four children to feed, an estate that was just starting to get on its feet... A whole life ahead.

Chapter IV

Leo was losing control of her life. Clemente sold himself as the ideal man, the one every woman would desire by her side, the knight who would never fail, who would always be there, steadfast in every moment of life, through good times and bad, and Leo bought into it. She thought he would be the person who would always be by her side until her eyes closed forever in the future, the man she needed to keep moving forward until the end. She envisioned herself surrounded by children and prosperity, everything a family represents, a legacy for life.

But sadly, a short time was determined to show her that this wasn't going to be the case: Clemente became a heavy burden on her shoulders. Clemente transformed into another disappointment in Leo's life, but she didn't want to fully accept it. Her love-stricken heart overpowered the reason in her mind; despite the extreme selfishness shown by Clemente and his exacerbated machismo, she believed she could change him, transform him into the man she thought was hidden deep within him.

Every day, the fights grew more intense, sometimes even without reason. Leo's sleepless nights waiting up late or until dawn for Clemente's return, who would come home reeking of alcohol, became a daily occurrence.

On one of those endless nights, waiting for him while seated by the window of the farmhouse, Clemente appeared very late, wanting to subdue Leo to unleash all his pent-up carnal fury from a night of revelry and alcohol. Leo shouted, thinking it was the moment to firmly say no, that she wouldn't do it with him, that she was tired of the situation. But the unexpected response she received was a hard blow that Clemente dealt to her right arm with a cudgel. That tough tool used by peasants to control animals made Leo realize that from now on she would be treated like this, like a beast that its tamer could handle as he pleased.

These increasingly frequent situations wore Leo down. She had ceased to be the strong woman everyone knew and had become a victim of Clemente. She couldn't understand how she was still with him, how she allowed those beatings without doing something to prevent them. She became submissive to the situation, letting time drag her along, and what she dreamt as a bright future slowly faded away, giving way to a toxic relationship from which she couldn't escape for a long time.

Leo's morale and self-esteem declined as the days went by. Those trade trips she was used to making became a thing of the past. Now she lived off what Clemente gave her, which was actually very little, almost nothing.

Searching for a way to survive, Leo decided to apply for a loan from the Agricultural Bank (Caja Agraria) to invest it and thus be able to better feed her children. Due to her good banking conduct, they didn't hesitate to grant it to her. Leo had an economic respite for a while, but later she felt the financial noose tightening around her neck again, unable to continue paying the bank's set installments, thus losing that financial aid. Leo's life had been reduced to enduring Clemente's snubs and humiliations and bearing children with him.

Amidst this terrible romantic and economic situation, a desperate Leo began to notice signs of a new pregnancy in her body. She couldn't believe it; she was devastated, but she had to press on.

Without finding solace, support, or a way out, she decided to go to the village church in search of enlightenment and the soothing balm she so desperately needed. She believed that by offering a fervent prayer, she would receive a response from the Creator. And so it was, God sent her a guardian angel dressed as a priest: Father Corredor.

Father Corredor and Leo formed a beautiful bond of friendship and support. He listened attentively to the laments of the depressed and lonely woman, responding with wise advice full of hope and faith about the future. But his help didn't stop there. In a gesture of immense nobility, Father Corredor further extended his hand to Leo by lending her money, which she invested in the purchase of three dairy cows for the farm.

Every dawn, Leo and her children would rise to milk the cows. The nutritious liquid obtained from the animals was divided into three parts: one for the house, one for sale, and one for Father Corredor, as a token of gratitude for being the only person who reached out to Leo when she needed it most.

The children would laugh heartily upon seeing the milk mustache that formed on Father Corredor's upper lip when he drank the milk. Knowing the tough situation the young members of the family were going through, he would make even more exaggerated faces, prompting even more laughter. Leo was at a loss for words to express her gratitude for these moments of joy.

Being the son of a financially stable couple, Clemente regularly received money from his parents, who also supported his behavior towards Leo. He, being a man skilled and charming in business, would invest this money in one quick venture or another, affording him the means to continue funding his nights of revelry, excesses, affairs, and alcohol, completely forgetting the responsibility he had to his partner and their unborn child. He didn't always sleep on the farm, and when he did, it was always at night, expecting Leo to have warm food ready for him on the table. Most of these nights, he would force her into intimate relations, threatening her with a brutal beating otherwise.

Leo was drained, no longer finding the strength to defend herself, her only concern being to protect her children and the baby growing inside her. Clemente had managed to diminish her both physically and morally. She didn't know how to break free from this life; she still held love for the image of that man, that tormentor who caused her so much pain, which is why she couldn't bring herself to leave or force him off the farm.

That woman who had found so much strength within herself to pull her family through despite the many blows life dealt her, began to succumb to depression and self-loathing, which is why her life remained unchanged.

On July 12, 1953, Yolanda was born. By then, Leo felt she no longer needed a midwife; she felt capable of welcoming her children into the world on her own. And so, she did. The little girl became her new beacon of light, but at the same time, her new source of worry.

But every once in a while, Leo experienced fleeting moments of joy. Over time, Alirio, her eldest son, was able to start attending a nearby school. He turned out to be a very good student and always exhibited exemplary behavior, despite the tumultuous and fractured home environment he was growing up in, surrounded by domestic violence.

Apart from this point of pride, monotony had firmly settled into Leo's life. Her eyes opened automatically every morning just to take care of her children, send Alirio to school, milk the cows, cook, and satisfy Clemente's sexual demands.

On January 20, 1955, Arbello was born, another child resulting from the sexual outbursts that took place in Leo's dream farmhouse. She now had six children to care for. Penniless and alone, she was trapped in the prison her life had become.

In the midst of her desperation to support her children and put food on the table, Leo decided to sell a small part of the farm that she loved so much to her neighbors. With that money, she managed to withstand the blows of hunger and her children's needs for a little while longer, during which time Clemente came and went without any concern or remorse for the state in which he had left his family. Without any shame or weight on his conscience, he began to sleep increasingly away from home, and after a few days, he would return to continue his reign of terror in the house.

Asariel, Leo's seventh child, was born on August 12, 1956. Leo and Clemente continued in their same routine. Nothing changed.

One might think that things would come to a head, but that wasn't the case, a fact that became evident one day when the neighbors felt compelled to call the police due to the screams coming from the property.

It turns out that the beating Clemente was giving Leo was so severe that the neighbors believed it might end in bloodshed or even death itself. However, when the police arrived at the location, Leo denied any assaults taking place inside the house, thus defending the father of her children and asking the officers to leave the premises.

The fight continued; the violence had reached a point of no return. Alirio, who was already eleven years old, remembered the moment when Clemente had injured his mother's arm, and without considering the consequences, lunged at Clemente. Like a wild animal, the boy grabbed the man from behind the neck with all his might, wrapping him with his small arm, trying to strangle him. Clemente shook him off like one would shake a leaf from a tree off their shoulder, and Alirio fell flat on the ground. He immediately got up, only to receive a powerful punch from Clemente, leaving him badly injured and leaning against a wall. Clemente fled the scene, running away as cowardly as his feet would allow him. He didn't return for several weeks, and when he did, it was only for a short while; he would only come occasionally to have fun with Leo, sex and food were the only things he sought on that property.

Leo sold another piece of the property. With much pain, she watched as it slowly transformed into a jigsaw puzzle of pieces that she gradually gave up just to survive. It was the only way left for her to provide for the household. Besides having to stay on the farm to take care of the children, her capabilities were further limited for a while due to the injury she had received on her arm, leaving a noticeable wound. Perhaps out of shame, or maybe due to lack of time, she didn't want to see a doctor for it. Thankfully, she had the help of her children, who under Leo's guidance gradually learned more about the daily tasks of running a household and a farm.

The event that broke the monotony of the days came when Eliseo and Yolanda, who were still very young, headed to the nearby well in search of fresh water to drink at home. Once standing at the edge of the well, Yolanda wanted to see how deep it was. Peering into the sheer black abyss below, she leaned further, slipped, and fell into the well. Eliseo didn't have time to catch her. It all happened so quickly; he couldn't believe it. One moment Yolanda was there, and in a matter of seconds, she had disappeared into the maw of a deep black hole.

Eliseo felt as if his legs were burning from the speed with which he ran home to find Leo. But she knew she wouldn't be able to do much with her arm in its current condition, so she quickly went to seek help from a neighbor. Juan, the owner of the neighboring farm, had already heard the commotion and was coming to the rescue. Together, the three rushed to the well. Anxiously, they peered in, unable to see anything, but they could hear Yolanda's cries from below. Juan took a rope that was nearby and threw it down, telling Yolanda to hold onto it with all her strength.

Yolanda felt her small hands burning from the force with which she was gripping the rope, but slowly, with each pull from Juan, she saw the light getting closer and closer until she was finally out. Pure joy. The girl had only a few scratches and a profound scare that settled deep in her gut.

Back at the house, Juan stayed with Leo for a while. It was clear that she was very shaken up from the fright she had just experienced, but in the midst of their conversation, feeling somewhat safe because of the supportive shoulder beside her, Leo released a flood of tears that had been held back for a long time. In that stream of tears, she let out days of fights, hits, and humiliations. She literally broke in two. Sitting on the chair, she leaned forward and, in a sort of exorcism, let out everything she was holding inside.

Juan, being a neighbor to the estate, already had a clear idea of what was happening inside the house. He extended his hand and took Leo's. She kept repeating that she was a prisoner, both of life and of a hostile, violent man. Juan told her what was obvious but she dared not see: she needed to leave that relationship at any cost or she'd end up dead and her children would be left orphans. She should be with a man who truly supported her, someone to erase Clemente from her life forever.

Those words stuck like nails in Leo's mind. For several months she tried to avoid Clemente, but it was impossible. His aggression made her mind, spirit, and body bend to his will. Just to avoid another beating, she would end up doing everything he told her to do. She was completely humiliated and dominated by him.

One afternoon, Leo went out alone to do some shopping, and during her walk, large tears streamed down her cheeks due to the recurring thought that drilled into her mind: what her life had become and how low she had fallen after being such an empowered woman and having survived all the challenges life had thrown at her.

An image of Miguelito appeared in her thoughts. An image emerging from the corridors of memories in her mind. She cried even harder, thinking about how she had lost even that child turned young man, that trusted lieutenant; he had disappeared from her life because of a man who was not worth it.

She pondered as she walked. She knew she was only moving for her children, the most important thing in her life, or rather the only important thing in her existence, because she even felt that her own life had no value. Leo had hit rock bottom.

She couldn't go on any longer and had to sit down on a bench in the village square. The tears wouldn't stop. She felt herself drying up inside, as if her skin would wither right there from the lack of fluid in her body. She buried her face in her hands and began to reflect on her life and the power of Juan's words: "You should be with a man who truly supports you."

Taking a deep breath, she rose from the bench to continue her journey to the market. Her steps were interrupted by a man of average height, with sharp features and a cigarette in hand, who asked if she was alright. Leo, surprised by how confidently the man had approached her, replied that yes, she was perfectly fine.

That man assured her that crying wasn't worth it, especially if she was the Doña Leo he had heard about. He knew who she was because he was from the area and had overheard in one conversation or another about the great woman who had bought the "El Cubo" estate. Strangely for Leo, since it was the first time she had seen this man, words flowed without any reservations. They talked for a long while, and Leo managed to get distracted from all her problems. And just like that, they said their goodbyes to continue on their respective paths. Leo thought about that stranger for a few blocks, about how odd it had been to talk openly with another man, a complete stranger to her, and even more so, to have a conversation different from the ones she had been having over the past years. She replayed the whole moment in her mind, remembering every word uttered until she reached his name... His name was Jesús.

That same afternoon, back at the estate, there was a knock at the entrance gate. To Leo's surprise, upon opening, she saw it was that audacious man with the cigarette, bearing a basket full of fruits he had bought at the market to gift her. She accepted them but did not let Jesús into the estate since he was a complete stranger. After a short while, Jesús said his goodbyes and left the same way he had come.

Juan was on his estate, observing everything that was happening. When Jesús had left, he approached Leo and asked, "Do you know Chucho?"

She, taken aback and surprised that Juan knew him, told him she had just met him that very day.

"You've been so wrapped up in your problems for so long that you no longer know the people of the village," Juan remarked. Then, lowering his voice, he said something that shocked Leo: "That's Chucho Cañón... He's wanted by the police. He's a dangerous man, and it's said that he's a murderer."

Leo stood frozen in place and time. A chill ran down her spine as she thought about the safety of her children and her own. Juan noticed and, in a somewhat jesting tone, added, "You could chase Clemente out of your life with Chucho's help..."

Leo smiled, not giving it much thought, but what she didn't know was that those words would be swirling in her head for the next few hours.

Jesús, better known as Chucho Cañón, returned to the estate the next day. Leo found herself in a slightly tense situation that tested her nerves. On one hand, deep down, she felt a certain fear that Clemente would return to the estate and find Chucho there. On the other hand, Juan's words still made her shiver. Here she was, talking and sharing with a man wanted by the law, a man many believed to be a murderer, yet in such a short time, he inspired a sense of security in her.

Little by little, they began a solid friendship. She had some reservations because of what Juan had told her, but practically speaking, she thought he might be her only way out with Clemente. After so many years, she was determined to do something to improve her life, no matter how insane or radical it sounded.

Time ensured that Leo and Chucho grew closer and closer. Their bond became stronger. Leo breathed the peace that Chucho's presence brought her, and she also found comfort in the fact that Clemente hadn't set foot on the estate for several weeks. One of those afternoons, during their conversations, Leo was completely honest with Chucho. She told him the story of her life and confessed that with him she felt a support and companionship that helped her feel better. It was there, at that moment, as they watched the sunset while seated on the porch of the house, that Chucho promised Leo he would always protect her.

A few days later, Clemente showed up at the estate with his airs of a husband who believed he owned and controlled everything. He entered through the main gate, shouting at the top of his lungs that the master of the estate had arrived and that they should treat him as such. He demanded to see Leo immediately. But the person who appeared, blocking his path, was none other than Jesús Chucho Cañón.

"Leo can't come out and doesn't want to at this moment," he stated authoritatively.

Clemente was taken aback; it had never crossed his mind that Leo could be with another man, let alone with Chucho Cañón, a criminal pursued by the town's police.

Gathering courage from his fear, Clemente confronted Chucho, saying that Leo was his woman and no one else's. To which Chucho replied in a threatening tone:

"Leo doesn't want to see you, and even less so do her children."

Clemente had no choice but to leave immediately, like a dog fleeing a confrontation with its tail between its legs.

Local folks say that Clemente tried to return to the estate on various occasions, but Chucho's threats, always present, grew increasingly potent, to the point that he told Leo he only needed her order to "murder and chop him up", ensuring he'd be rid of him for good.

Finally, Clemente got the message: it was either to continue his obsession, indulging in moments of lust with Leo's body, or to face imminent death in the attempt. Yes, it was better to leave, to forget her, to find another victim whose life he could shatter... He went away, and Clemente never returned.

Chucho, the children, and Leo had a well-deserved peaceful time within the walls of the farmhouse, far from arguments and physical and psychological abuse. At last, the children began to be happy. Leo couldn't understand why people thought Jesus was a bad man, a murderer, when it had been so long since she felt this way, with such peace and tranquility, since it had been a long time since a man treated her the way she deserved.

It is presumed that it was Clemente himself who informed the police that Chucho Cañón was at the farm, thus ending the peace that reigned in the place. Word quickly spread to the relatives of those murdered by Chucho, who demanded justice from the police. Yes, he was a fugitive, and that could endanger his children, but Leo felt committed to him and thought she could not abandon him, as this man had helped her in the worst moment of her life and she should do the same for him. She believed that, even though he was a murderer and a fugitive, he was a better person and treated her better than Clemente ever had.

For several nights, they had to sleep in the woods, an event the children saw as an adventure under the stars. They often returned to the farm to eat and gather supplies, but without lighting even a single candle or peeking through a window. No one, not even Juan, could find out they were in the house until things calmed down.

Despite the entire situation, Alirio never stopped his studies or stopped attending school. Leo always managed to ensure this, no matter where they were. It never crossed her mind to deprive her children of an education. She believed that everyone should be educated and succeed with the little help she could provide.

Internally, she became a more submissive person, but her ideas were very clear. She believed she was gradually emerging from the hole she found herself in, even while being with a criminal.

Aware of all the problems Leo was going through, her neighbors began advising her to leave the area, to sell whatever remained of the farm, and use that money to move to Bogotá, Chiquinquirá, or any other place to start a quieter life from scratch. A place where Chucho wouldn't have problems. With such advice, they also took the opportunity to try and get him out of that area, which had become dangerous because of his presence.

Leo began to consider it. Alirio, her eldest son, had already completed his primary studies, and she managed to enroll him in the Industrial School of Chiquinquirá, securing lodging for him in a house in the area. All of this was to give a brighter future to a boy as brilliant as he was, distancing him a bit from the problems and worries they faced at home. This also encouraged Leo to move, so she could be closer to her son.

Sadly, due to all the scandals that had occurred on the farm and her romantic relationship with a man on the run from the law, Leo lost the reputation she had worked so hard to build. Both the residents of neighboring farms and those from the town constantly talked about her life. Behind her back, countless stories circulated about her close relationship with Chucho Cañón and how he drove Clemente out of her life. Leo had become the mandatory topic of conversation at gatherings.

Knowing this situation, Leo became fully convinced to sell the farm and the few animals she had left. By twists of fate, that law of attraction to things from the past, the deal was closed with Tomás Cortez, a relative of Clemente who had learned about the situation. During the transaction, there was no event or approach between Leo and Clemente. She feared a new scandal if the father of her children and Chucho met again, so she avoided at all costs that this would happen.

Once again, Leo packed up her things and those of her children to embark on a new journey. It seemed her life was destined to close and open cycles over and over again. To get her hopes up, live it, abandon it, mourn it, and leave it behind. Another piece of land was lost behind her with each step she took leaving. The family grew, and more hands clung to hers... She had to keep moving forward for her children. Another path to face alone, for now, as Jesús would catch up with them after some time. He first needed to throw the police off his trail.

Once settled in Chiquinquirá, a city, a modern place with a bustling life, far removed from what she had experienced with her children in the countryside, Leo set up a small commercial business, which lasted only a short time. The money she received wasn't enough to support her family, which was now set to grow even more. Yes, inside Leo's womb grew a child of Jesús Chucho Cañón.

Now, if the departure from the farm had been lonely, her new life would be even lonelier. A day before Chucho was to come to Chiquinquirá, he heard dogs barking from his hideout. He peeked out the window and saw police officers stealthily approaching. He quickly grabbed his things and escaped through the back door of his hideaway, rushing into the woods. The police started running after him. After a few minutes, Chucho felt the embrace of freedom, looking back and seeing no officers nearby. He kept running with a smile, not noticing a tree root protruding in his path. He tripped, fell, and screamed from the pain of his leg, broken in three places. It was only a few minutes before the officers reached him. Chucho was arrested. They took him away in handcuffs. Images of Leo and their children waiting for him flashed through his mind. Fate's cruel hand dealt its ugliest cards once more. The news hit Leo like a dagger piercing her stomach.

Diving into a new venture, starting a business completely unknown to her, Leo decided to open a small restaurant in front of the Chiquinquirá market square. It was small but very cozy, primarily serving fried food and selling beer.

Dairo de Jesús was born on September 3, 1959. Chucho, his father, had been found guilty of murder and was to spend at least twenty-five years behind bars. He was transferred to a maximum-security prison in the Department of Boyacá, and once again, Leo was left alone with a newborn in her arms.

As the days passed, the restaurant began to decline. The few customers who came didn't feel entirely well-served or often found it closed when they arrived. Leo had to take care of the new baby, get the older children to school, look after the others, and manage the business. By now, Leo had eight children. It was a highly complicated situation.

In Chiquinquirá, she didn't have a place of her own; she wasn't in the countryside anymore. The city was very different; everything had to be bought, she couldn't grow anything. She had run out of money, and that's how she started thinking of Celina, her older sister. Celina could be her only help, her salvation, since she was married to a man who was doing well financially. She was her only hope, she thought.

One morning, she heard a knock at her door. It was the landlord, bringing the bad news: if they didn't pay the rent immediately, they would have to pack their things and leave.

Leo was broken both financially and physically. With a constant, piercing pain in her arm from the unhealed injury, she couldn't continue with the restaurant. Without money and with eight mouths to feed, for the first time in her life, she didn't know what to do. In utter misery, she found herself on the street, asking for work. She managed to clean and wash in some houses just to eat.

Every night, in complete solitude, almost fainting from exhaustion, she thought about how her relationship with Clemente had ruined her life.

Chapter V

Leo's desperation and distress grew with each passing day, evident in the dark circles now etched under her eyes, a result of countless sleepless nights searching for a moment's rest. She was no longer herself, unable to find solace amidst the overwhelming troubles.

She couldn't bear it any longer, she couldn't endure another day submerged in this situation, so she decided to call her sister Celina, seeking help. The call was made early. Her words were slow, soaked in tears of despair and pain. Gradually, she painted the bleak picture for her sister, describing her dire circumstances. To this, Celina responded with astonishment and concern, assuring her that she was willing to help and suggesting that Leo and her family come to Bogotá as soon as possible, where she would welcome them with open arms.

Thank God, a safe shore was now in sight. However, there remained one last hurdle before reaching this safe haven: Leo had to find the means to make the move, a journey with seven young children who had left school to head to an unknown place. Alirio would stay in Chiquinquirá to complete his studies at the industrial school.

Leo still retained her financial savvy, and through sales and transactions, she managed to gather the funds necessary for the move. Early in the morning, a truck was already waiting for them, into which they loaded the few possessions they had. Among these, everyone settled in as best they could. Leo knew they faced many hours on the road, cramped among household items, boxes, and bags of clothes. And so, once again, this family embarked on another move, another journey, another quest for a brighter future. Leaving the pain and troubles behind, letting them burn in the fires of the past, hoping those ashes would never again be lifted by the wind.

Upon finally arriving in the Claret neighborhood, an area not very luxurious, where Celina had lived with her husband for several years, they felt a great relief. At last, they could stretch their bodies after getting off the truck. The couple, with kind smiles, awaited them at the door of what would be a new refuge, a place to gather their thoughts and start a new life.

They were offered the only available space in the home, a small room on the rooftop, which was accessed by a somewhat dangerous ladder, especially for the children who would now live there. But they gradually adapted, eventually climbing up and down with great skill. This little room would be, for a while, the new place where they'd spend their days and dream at night. Leo kept reminding them that they were only passing through, that it would be for a short time while the situation improved.

And so the days on the calendar began to roll by.

Unfortunately, the children couldn't continue their school courses that year since the school period was already well underway. They had to wait several months, with not much to do, until the start of a new school year.

For her part, Leo, without wasting much time, began to look for work. She decided to return to what she knew best, and one morning she woke up with the idea of going immediately to the Claret neighborhood market, and so she did. Once there, she sharpened all her senses to absorb as much information as possible. She wanted to understand how trading was done in the area, how the economy moved, and what was the best way to start making money immediately with the products sold there.

That same day, she also visited Plaza España, located at Carrera 19 crossing with Avenida Jiménez, which was the largest market in Bogotá. Leo noticed that it was a much bigger space, and with the little money she had, she seized the opportunity and bought cheeses, blackberries, and other fruits to immediately resell them.

Thus, without wasting time, Leo began the routine that in previous years had brought her satisfaction and money. The difference now was that she had to leave the children alone all day. It didn't take long for Celina to become irritated. They were small children left alone in a tiny rooftop room, and a warning alarm echoed in her conscience every now and then. The alarm only silenced when she checked on them.

Thus the months went by, and little by little, Leo managed to earn money for food. Her contacts in the market grew. Every day she got to know more and more people. This was her routine; this was her daily life. If she maintained this pace, her children would always have food on the table.

Margarita, Isaura, Eliseo, and Yolanda, the older children, started school. The younger ones, Arbello, Asariel, and Jesús would usually wait at home until Leo arrived. Even though they were the youngest, she always prepared them to face any situation, constantly explaining and urging them above all else not to bother their Aunt Celina. By this time, Leo began to notice that her sister didn't entirely approve of how she was making a living. While Celina acknowledged that it was an honorable way to provide for her children, she didn't agree with the idea that children should fend for themselves. She believed more in the notion that there was always a solution, that children shouldn't spend much of their day away from their mother.

The people that Leo had contacts with for doing business in the market gradually became her friends. She began to feel that she hadn't fully lived her youth like most women, always being under the pressure of responsibility towards her family, a job… always having someone under her care. There was always someone depending on her. She felt there was nothing wrong with, every now and then, after a workday, going with her friends to the local bars to have some beers and relax. At first, it was a kind of escape, but unfortunately, these escapes became excessive. They happened more and more often.

Eliseo, who was now eleven, began to notice that when he returned from school, his mom was never in the rooftop room, and on his own initiative, he started going to the market to look for her, without her realizing. He wanted to know more about his mother's work and her life outside of home, which led to a growing overprotective sense towards Leo within him.

As the days went by, a man named Manuel began to notice Eliseo's presence in the market. He watched as the boy sat under a canopy, observing people passing by, when in reality, he was tracking his mother's movements. This man offered him a job. Now, after attending school, Eliseo could earn some money selling the bananas that Manuel provided him around the market area. It was a job that lasted only a few weeks, but he could still watch what his mother was doing. It was a task he undertook with fear of being discovered, but he preferred to be there than locked up within four small walls taking care of all his younger siblings. He felt it wasn't fair.

Eliseo began to notice that Leo worked until one or two in the afternoon, and then she would go with her friends to the bar. He, being a protective son with a determined character, began to follow her and wait for her every day at the door of the liquor establishments, just to prevent any inebriated man from bothering her or to ensure she didn't get into any trouble while intoxicated. The first few times Leo noticed Eliseo acting as a protective shadow, she took it as a sweet gesture from her son. However, as time went on, they began to argue. Leo definitely wouldn't let herself be controlled by a child. Their arguments became increasingly heated, but still, Eliseo never stopped following her, even if she got angry and even hit him to stop him from monitoring her.

After a while, the local authorities decided to relocate the market from Plaza España, due to the proximity of the traffic offices. The noise from the bustling commercial activity every morning made it difficult for the government office to operate. The market was moved to a place called Palo Quemado, which was simply a large pasture.

This new location brought about certain changes in the activity. One of them was that the selling spots would no longer be set up daily; on the contrary, the market would only open its doors two or three times a week, which meant a change in Leo's routine and income. However, undeterred by the situation, she noticed that in Palo Quemado, being a pasture, they also sold pigs, chickens, and cows. She saw this as a new opportunity and decided to buy animals with the intention of reselling them to make more money.

Leo continued working diligently. Every day, without rest, she carried out her economic activities, which usually kept her busy until mid-afternoon. Then, at the end of the day, she felt she deserved that much-coveted drink that loosened the knots of responsibility a bit... She didn't realize it, didn't feel it, and it never crossed her mind, but Eliseo was her daily shadow. Yes, Leo was becoming an alcoholic.

Even though Leo worked every day, her trips to the bars began to cloud her judgment and perspective. Food started to become scarce at home; there wasn't enough anymore. This situation made the absence of a mother even more acute for the children: youngsters without food and without a present maternal figure. Without time for lamentations, they began to fend for themselves. They were simply on their own, and that's how they became a team, a family that had to push forward no matter what, coming up with daily solutions to meet their needs. Isaura and Margarita managed in the kitchen; Eliseo assisted his younger siblings as best he could, and sometimes they took turns with responsibilities.

But it wasn't enough. Many times the team made up of children failed. They would go to school without eating or bathing, looking dirty and unkempt. Still, they managed to get by and complete their school years. What truly drove them to persevere was Leo's fixation on education. They came to see it as an obsession of their mother's, but much later, in the subsequent years, deep down they would be grateful for it. For Leo, that was the only thing that mattered in that house. Despite the circumstances, the children never stopped studying. They feared their mother's threats if they were ever absent or if they failed the school year.

Many times, the children received help from neighbors and teachers who pitied the precarious situation that was reflected in the children's clothes, eyes, and physical constitution. But when that wasn't the case, when the adults couldn't help, they continued to share responsibilities that children shouldn't have to bear. The older siblings always looked out for their younger brothers and sisters.

But no, the help from the neighbors wasn't enough, the kind hand of the teachers was insufficient.

One day, in great hunger and desperation, Eliseo looked into his siblings' eyes and couldn't bear it any longer. He went out into the street in search of something to eat. After walking a few blocks, he saw a truck loaded with bananas parked on the side of the street. Without thinking of the consequences, with a stomach growling from hunger and the memory of his little siblings' complaints, he climbed onto the back of the truck and started grabbing bananas and hiding them under his shirt. As he was about to grab the fifth banana, he felt a large, strong hand grasp his wrist. It was the truck owner, who had seen what the boy was doing. Without any compassion, he slapped Eliseo, a sharp open-handed blow that stirred the boy's deepest emotions.

He thought of his siblings' tears of hunger, that he had been pushed to steal because of his mother's absence. He hated alcohol with all his being, that liquid that day by day took more and more of his mother away from him. He ran down the street with his swollen cheek throbbing in pain, a pain only comparable to the memory of Leo getting intoxicated daily with beer and other drinks offered to her in the taverns. Yes, his mother had lost her way. For her, her children's food and well-being were no longer important. She was not the same responsible woman she used to be.

Something broke inside Eliseo. His soul aged hundreds of years from the blow he received from the truck driver. The fights with Leo became more frequent and fierce, battles that only filled him with more helplessness, as, due to his young age, he always ended up losing them.

To further complicate matters, Leo began a romantic relationship with a man named Daniel. He looked bad, was dirty, had vices, and was ill-mannered. It was to be expected that the children did not like his presence at all. However, Leo still invited him to spend more and more time in that small rooftop room. Her older children did their best to get him out, but Daniel seemed not to care, leading the fights between Eliseo and Leo to escalate even more.

Leo and Daniel had the terrible routine of getting drunk daily in the bars and then coming home to continue drinking. One day, Eliseo, blinded by rage, reached a point of no return. Daniel's presence in the room was unbearable and it awakened in the boy a feeling that, for grown men, was punishable by earthly, spiritual, and moral laws. His childlike innocence would be erased forever: he went to his Aunt Celina's house, took a jar of insecticide, returned to the small room, and poured a large stream of the poisonous liquid into a plate of soup that Leo had prepared only for Daniel. Fortunately, as if in a suspense movie, the unkempt man loudly stated that he had to leave the room immediately to go to the market, without even taking a single spoonful of the wicked concoction. Eliseo felt as if the whole universe was conspiring against him, not realizing that Daniel's departure had saved even his own life. He had no choice but to, unbeknownst to his mother, pour the poisoned soup down the toilet.

One day, Celina realized that her sister could not continue living in such a small space with so many children. She also thought that a change would give Leo a new direction, something to regain her bearings in her life and that of her children. With this in mind, she offered Leo a small lot of her property so that she could, with her own hands and effort, build a larger place to live with her children. Without giving it much thought, Leo accepted her sister's proposal and arranged everything for a new move as soon as possible, obtaining pieces of cardboard, newspapers, and wood, materials that for the most part Celina's husband gifted them to help raise a small and humble shack.

Shortly before the move, Doña Mariel, the paternal grandmother of Leo's two daughters with José: Margarita and Isaura, paid a visit. This lady, seeing the precarious conditions in which they lived, expressed to Leo her wish to take the two girls back to the countryside. At first, Leo was wary of the idea, but after some thought, she agreed, knowing that as strong as she might feel, the girls would be better off with their grandmother in a larger house, and surrounded by family affection, the kind that was gradually being lost within the four walls of a tiny room on the roof of a house.

Isaura was not in agreement with this plan. Responding to her childlike instincts, she decided to stay with her mom and siblings without fully understanding what her grandmother was offering her. One morning, Margarita left holding her grandmother's hand, taking one last look at the room she was certain she wouldn't miss in the future. She wanted to forget all the arguments and bad times she lived there. She didn't want to remember that it was in that place that her mom stopped being her mother and became that strange and gloomy being who only came home to scold and mistreat them. She didn't mind the fact that she'd never step into a school again; for the rest of her life, she felt quite comfortable with country life... and nothing beyond that.

Including Leo and the children, they were now seven. Once the humble shack they built with their own hands was somewhat livable, they moved in.

This new home was a bit larger than the room they came from. It had one single room, one bed where they all had to sleep squeezed together. There were many differences, but one that bothered the children most was the dirt floor, as their feet were always dirty now. If it rained, water seeped through the gaps in the cardboard and wood, and the home ceased to be a home, turning into a big mud puddle. And if it was very sunny, the floor turned into desert sand. They didn't have running water or a bathroom. They didn't have a table or chairs... There were many things they once had and now didn't. Everyone knew it wasn't a good change, but Leo was happy not to have to endure the scoldings from her sister Celina, who, with increasing frequency, chastised her for her behavior and the loneliness of her children.

Within a few days, Celina began to show that, even though she had offered them a place to live on their own, deep down she was wary of her property. She started to fear that Leo might take over the land, especially with Daniel and his bad habits coming into her life. But Leo always assured her this would not be the case and that she was, on the contrary, grateful for the help they were receiving from both Celina and her husband.

Daniel continued visiting Leo regularly until one day he showed up at the ranch's door carrying a mattress. The children watched in astonishment as this man, overnight, began living with them, sleeping with their mother in the same bed. Despite all their objections and reservations, this situation had come to stay in their lives.

The couple continued their alcohol-soaked routine. Every morning they disappeared and returned late at night, completely intoxicated. The children, more and more alone, increasingly hungry, while Leo, happy with the freedom she felt she so deserved (according to her own words), voiced this every time a child confronted her.

One night, shouts from men fighting awoke the children and neighbors. Two shadows approached and pushed each other at the ranch's door. A frenzied dance of feet dodging and jumping raised a cloud of dust that, combined with the darkness, made it hard to discern what was happening. Yells and insults. Two voices claiming possession of a woman, until everything fell silent. A line of blood traced the ground, and the dust began to settle. Neighbors went in search of the police. The officers arrived to unravel the mystery: Daniel was fighting with another man who was pursuing Leo. The one lying on the ground had an injured hand, and standing next to him was Daniel, wielding a bloodied knife. The children heard everything. They saw the blood and the wound. They felt their life shattering even more. Where was mom at that moment?

Surprisingly, mom was telling the police not to arrest anyone, that neither man was at fault, that it was just a misunderstanding fueled by rum and beer.

Everything continued as usual. Eliseo and Isaura began to go to the market in the evenings to pick up pieces of yucca, potato, orange, or any food from the ground to feed their siblings. They rummaged through trash bags looking for something to eat, and to avoid walking long distances on empty stomachs, they would sneak onto buses and trucks.

Leo would return to the ranch around eleven or midnight, and some nights she didn't return at all. The neighbors noticed the situation and alerted the authorities. However, when interviewed by the police, Leo always denied the allegations. She explained that whenever she went to work, the children were watched over by an adult like her sister Celina or some acquaintance passing through the area. She stated that she left them alone because of her job, and that it was the only way to make ends meet quickly. Every time this happened, Leo would change: she would come home earlier, pay a little more attention to the children. But after a while, she would revert back, falling into a cycle of vice and excess.

All the responsibilities unfit for a child of his age fell upon Eliseo. Being the eldest male, he was always the most responsible. In reality, both Leo and life itself had indirectly taught him to be aware of everything around him and to try to keep things afloat for the sake of the family. For instance, ensuring that both he and his siblings never missed school and didn't neglect their tasks, despite all the hardships they were experiencing at the time. He often managed these challenges with the help of his teachers, who were aware of the situation at home.

Despite the exhaustion from so many responsibilities, he continued trying to prevent his mother from leading the life she was living. Bitterly, he would hold up her misbehavior as an example for his sisters, urging them to always choose the right path in life and to never become like their mother.

One night, Eliseo, stripped of all childlike innocence and hardened by life's trials, followed Leo to a hotel where she went with a man who wasn't Daniel. He waited for her to come out, not to reprimand her, but to make her see the error of her ways. And yet, through all this, he still wanted to protect and help her escape her dissolute life. Almost every night, he wept from anger and helplessness, but he persisted, following her like a protective shadow, holding onto the hope that things would change someday.

Eliseo's days were spent studying, taking care of his siblings, searching for food, and watching over his mother. Dirty and hungry, he would scour his body for the energy to do the same things every day, in a shack where there was no water. Several times a week, a neighbor would pass a hose over so they could collect a bit of liquid and take a bath. That same neighbor, taking pity on the children, would set up a television for them to watch through the bars of his house. Those days when they could watch TV through the gaps were special days. They would sit for hours in front of the bars, trying to watch some show broadcasted by that magical box that momentarily lifted them out of their sad and grim reality. On other occasions, when there was no television, joy came from the little food the neighbors gave them out of pity.

Leo only came home to sleep, she didn't even shower anymore, and she didn't help with chores or anything; she didn't even care if they had managed to get something to eat or not, she was only focused on working to spend it all on alcohol. Neighbors and even teachers helped the children with notebooks and pencils so they wouldn't miss school. It was a very tough time, a life of abysmal misery.

Leo excused her neglect of her children by the fact that she never let them miss school. Maybe this was the only thing that mattered to her; the kids could never miss class, under any circumstance, or they would have to face her wrath. But this was utterly contradictory when, many times, the young children wet the bed and neither Leo nor anyone else cleaned them up... going to school smelling of urine.

Everything changed when one day, out of the blue, like some kind of angel, a neighbor offered Leo a house with a restaurant so that she and her children could move and have a better life.

The rent for the place was very low, and even though she hadn't had much luck with that kind of business before, in a moment of clarity, she thought the offer could be a good idea to provide a better quality of life for her children, and for her to change her environment and try to quit drinking.

All of this had to be seen. An opportunity for change, real and lasting change. To rise to the surface again. To reach the pinnacle of life once more, the balancing of the scales. But, for this to happen, there were burdens to let go of, heavy anchors that prevented sailing towards the horizon... Daniel was still around and still in her life.

Chapter VI

A new house, a new business, a new promise of a stable future for her and her children. Leo had in front of her eyes a new opportunity. She was one step away from either saving her life or falling into an abyss she'd never emerge from, mired in the mud of alcohol and detachment from things that truly mattered. Deep down, she knew perfectly well that she was not on the right path, and that Daniel's company only harmed her existence.

Her children were growing. Besides a new work opportunity, a change of environment would be good for everyone. The house they were offered was old, but much larger than the cramped place they were currently living in, where they didn't even have separate rooms. It looked promising: a place to work and live comfortably, a place to improve their lives forever.

In the few moments when alcohol didn't cloud Leo's judgment, she could only think of leaving and forgetting everything, especially Daniel, who was driving her further and further away from her children. Should she continue with his bad influence, risking her children getting lost in life, or reclaim the love of her family and distance herself from Daniel forever? The answer was clear, simple, like cards on the table.

In those lucid moments, Leo knew that men and alcohol had been the cursed components that made her lose her way in life. And definitely, Daniel had not been a lifesaver; on the contrary, that bad man quickly became an anchor tied to her neck, a heavy weight pulling her uncontrollably into an extremely dark ocean.

One morning, without giving it further thought, she accepted the proposal from that neighbor, that angel who appeared in the middle of her path, who unknowingly had saved her life. Once again, they had to move, cleanse themselves from the wounds of failure, and head out on the road with their sights set on a promising future... Without giving much explanation to the children, she asked them to help her pack the few things they had, to leave the place without saying goodbye or looking back.

It was a blind departure, as Leo had not seen the place they were heading to. Only hope kept her vision clear. So, with just the knowledge that the house was bigger, she was convinced that it would be her new refuge. A place to lay new foundations for her family.

Taking advantage of the fact that Mr. Manuel, the owner of the house, was an old friend of her sister Celina, Leo agreed on the first payment with the little she had. He saw in Leo a dual opportunity: he could help a family that truly needed a roof over their heads, and in doing so, he would have someone to take care of that old house which had been abandoned and forgotten for many years. Leo and her children seemed to him very good candidates to maintain and care for it, as a building of its age deserved.

And so, one afternoon they left the small shack, hastily, like fugitives escaping from a past that, if they ran fast enough, wouldn't catch up with them and all its negativity. Leo fled from alcohol and bad company. She quickened her pace, fearing that Daniel might show up at any moment just to prevent her departure, poisoning her with alcohol and the typical promises of a wayward man whose only justification for existence was to harm a woman.

Leo invested all her energy into recovering her entrepreneurial spirit that she had discarded in the past due to decisions she shouldn't have made. She explained to her children, by way of apology, that they were heading for a better life, that everything would change, and that the familial love, which the children so sorely missed, would once again flourish in every corner of their new home, and soon they'd be a team like they once were.

To achieve this, she knew she had to stay away from alcohol completely, a herculean task since she was deeply hooked on that poison. But she didn't let herself be defeated. She clung to the hope of a new beginning and, little by little, with all her might, she replaced the bottle in her hand with the joy of a new future.

Everyone began to settle into their new home, a new house where everyone would now have rooms and beds to sleep soundly. They had running water and a roof that wouldn't let cascades of cold water pour in when it rained. Happiness was reborn on everyone's faces, and it wasn't long before they forgot the bad times of the past, no matter how significant they were. In the innocence of the children, there was no room for resentment.

Like alcohol, which manifested itself from time to time in Leo's withdrawal, Daniel also appeared in her daily thoughts. Yes, even though he was an extremely bad man, she couldn't deny that she missed him. Until one day, she realized that he too had become a bad habit. Leo deployed all her powers of forgetting the negatives in her life and clung to the conviction of improving and growing again. Only in this way could she forget so much poison.

Just days after arriving at the new house, Leo spoke to Isaura and Yolanda, the older girls, and explained to them that they would soon start helping her prepare meals. They needed to pay close attention and put all their effort into learning the kitchen's crafts. The urgency was due to the fact that on the streets surrounding the house, workers passed by heading to nearby construction sites. It was an opportunity to start selling, to offer delicious meals to the workers and gradually make themselves known, and later open a dining area in a part of the house suitable for that purpose.

The girls' excitement was twofold: they could finally spend time with their mother, whom they had missed so much, and they would learn a trade that could serve them later in life. Although with the move, the school was now farther away, they promised their mother that they would accompany her to the market to shop. And so they did, as soon as they left school, they hurried home to help their mother delightedly.

At home, everything began to take its course. The boys and girls went to school, while Leo stayed home putting the finishing touches so that when they returned, they would immediately start preparing delicious stews.

Every member of the family had their responsibility within the gears of the business. Each one contributed, which gave them satisfaction, and at the same time, they learned the trades of both the kitchen and commerce, each adding their personal touch. Leo's idea bore fruit, as more and more workers gradually joined the orders, and in a short time, they began to gain a reputation in the area.

As time passed, the business began to bring in financial rewards, so much so that Leo was able to hire two girls who lived near the house to help Isaura and Yolanda, while she focused on finding ways to expand the reputation they had all built together. She was like an ant, restless and never content staying in one place earning the same amount with just one job.

In an effort to stay as far away from the markets as possible, to avoid falling back in with the bad company of those she had once called friends, Leo began to venture into poultry farming, buying and selling domestic fowl. She started by purchasing twenty hens from a small farm. In order to transport and then sell them, she craftily placed them in cloth sacks and discreetly took them on public transport, praying she wouldn't get caught, as drivers didn't allow animals on their buses.

The day came when she thought it would be better to buy the birds in the company of Eliseo, so that he could act as a distraction on the transport vehicles. And that's exactly what happened: the young man would board the bus, distracting the driver with youthful antics while Leo would sneak past him with a sack full of chickens. Upon reaching their destination, they would burst into laughter, knowing they had shared in a delightful mischief. This was something that Eliseo greatly enjoyed, as he felt reconnected with his true mother; not the woman who had reached a point of not recognizing him during her drunken states.

Leo was impressed by how easily that business went. She was truly amazed at how she could buy between twenty and forty chickens in the morning, and by the afternoon she didn't have a single one left to sell. Reselling chickens turned out to be a completely profitable business for her, and it also brought two more benefits: it kept her completely away from the taverns by keeping her body and mind busy, and it brought her closer to her guardian son, Eliseo.

She, along with her son, began analyzing the pig market. Her sons became her new advisors. They thought it would be as successful as the chicken business, so they took a risk and bought two pigs. Using the leftover food from the restaurant, they fed and fattened them in the yard of the large house, and then resold them in the fields. Yes, it was an easy and lucrative business.

Soon they acquired more pigs. Eliseo and Arbello, after school, went with wheelbarrows to larger restaurants to ask for leftover food, and with what they got, they fed the pigs. Gradually, the restaurant business took a backseat, as the resale of animals was bringing in much more money.

Leo's life underwent a complete change. Now, her only company was her children; her family finally became the most important thing in her life. She realized in a short time that distancing herself from alcohol and bad men was the best decision she had ever made, something that, had she not done so, would have weighed on her for the rest of her life.

Leo's vision came to the forefront again. She realized that without her own means of transportation, her financial life would remain stagnant. She didn't mind going into debt when she bought a 1954 Ford truck, even if she didn't know how to drive it. She hired a driver and began transporting up to three hundred chickens a day for resale. That's how she started selling wholesale, and in this way, she managed to pay off the truck in a short time. She was overjoyed. She was achieving the stability she had dreamed of without having to drag along the burden of a man who wouldn't let her thrive.

For a long time, she continued like this, working non-stop, taking care of her children, ensuring they were always in school, and raising them to be good children, always valuing hard work and good manners.

Another investment opportunity came Leo's way. An acquaintance couple decided to move to the United States, leaving a small lot for sale in a middle-class area. Leo bought it with installment payments, as she had always done in her life, since luck always seemed to favor her in that regard. Brick by brick, she began to build a small house on the land. Another success in Leo's renewed journey. Another sign that she was on the right path in life.

For his part, Alirio graduated from school in Chiquinquirá and immediately started a course and a part-time job. Even though he rarely saw his mother or siblings, he always looked out for his family, even helping Leo with some money for her siblings' school expenses.

One by one, the pieces in Leo's life fell into place. Harmony and peace had returned to her days, and for the first time in a long time, she could sleep through the night. She was different, radiant, and undoubtedly well-rested.

Thanks to these economic improvements, one day Leo sent Eliseo and Isaura to Boyacá to find their sister Margarita, who was still living in their grandmother's house. Upon arriving, her siblings were surprised to see that Margarita was no longer a child, but she still acted like one, since she had never attended any school and had dedicated her short life to helping her grandmother with household chores. The old lady knew that this day would come; she was prepared for her family to show up and claim another member of their core family. Therefore, without any hesitation, she agreed to let Margarita go with her siblings.

The bricks of Leo's life were now complete. At last, she was in harmony, surrounded by her family, everything proceeding according to the new life plan she had sketched for herself in the stars of the future.

They all continued studying and helping Leo in raising chickens, pigs, and now cows, which they began to buy and keep in a small pen they built in the house's backyard. From early in the morning, Leo applied all the advice she had learned from her beloved father, teachings that her children gradually absorbed. Every day she was grateful for having learned so much from him, and she felt even more pride seeing that this knowledge was, at the moment, the greatest treasure her children were inheriting. Now, with her older children, she received more help at home and felt less weight on her shoulders.

During the time they were in the big house, Leo always sought a way to buy it. She really liked the area where it was located, but that very fact made its price considerably high. Therefore, she had to settle with continuing to pay the rent on time, as they had their little farm with various animals there. Meanwhile, she was slowly building a house on her new land, which was a significant expense.

Against all odds, on the new plot, a single-story house was finally constructed. When it was ready, Leo sold the animals and, accompanied by her family, made the last move they would make for quite some time.

Once settled, everyone gave their best to ensure peace and harmony continued to reign in their environment.

Leo, always with her vision projected far beyond the future, understood that, now that she had a plot in her name, something of her own that provided shelter, she could invest again with minimal risk. After some time, she decided to buy the neighboring plot, which was empty, with no construction on it. Slowly, over the course of the following years, she managed to build two three-story houses on each of the plots, which she merged into one. But she didn't stop there. Seven years passed, during which she added another floor to each, and transformed them into very comfortable apartments.

Yes, the pieces of life's puzzle finally fit together in Leo's existence. She breathed life's oxygen surrounded by her beloved children. She was a full-time mother, with the meaning and weight that each letter that forms the word 'mom' carries.

The life of her children, who by then were no longer young kids, changed dramatically. Gone were the days of hunger, misery, and distress. The Leo who frequented taverns and lost her way in life due to poor choices in men was now far behind. At last, they celebrated holidays in their home like any other family. Christmas was always eagerly anticipated by everyone, as Leo spared no expense in giving beautiful gifts and colorful clothes to each of her children. The long-desired time of stability and abundance had come to the Peña family... They were finally happy.

When Eliseo entered his teenage years, nearing the end of school, Leo managed to buy a car for him to have, making life at home more comfortable. Although she didn't know how to drive, she found a way to accomplish her goal, and little by little, her son learned the art of driving somewhat empirically. Eliseo gladly took on the responsibility of doing the shopping, running errands, and driving his younger siblings to school. He certainly was a big help.

Although Eliseo's presence in the house was irreplaceable, Leo couldn't stop thinking that her ever-present guardian angel needed to continue with his studies. She knew he should go to university, just like all his siblings would at some point in life. Yes, each would be missed at home and in Leo's heart, but given everything they had been through, her children needed to be prepared for the workforce that awaited them. She didn't want, for anything in the world, for her children to go back to the hardship they had already overcome.

Leo never stood still; it simply wasn't in her nature to sit and watch life go by without doing anything. She was always analyzing business opportunities, something that would surpass everything she had done up to that point. This time, she decided to buy two trucks and hire a couple of drivers to operate them. With these acquisitions, she could transport more animals, which meant increased profits for the household. But she didn't stop there; over time, she bought a bus and immediately put it to work, transporting passengers through the streets, avenues, and roads of the area. Everything brought in dividends.

On the other hand, she always had in the back of her mind the implicit debt she owed to her sister Celina for letting them stay at her house in Bogotá, a help that was invaluable when they needed it most. So, without further ado, Leo decided to reach out to her and suggest that her son Victor come and work at her house for a while as a way of showing gratitude. Both agreed, and this led to a long and fruitful working relationship.

Now that everything had improved and was going smoothly, Leo told her son Alirio that it was no longer necessary for him to keep sending money for his siblings. Everything he had done for them was already more than enough, and there were no treasures or castles on earth that could repay so much assistance.

On a sunny day, early in the morning, there was a loud knock on the door. Leo opened it, driven by curiosity, only to find herself face to face with Alirio, who had returned home as a surprise. He had completed all his courses and studies away from the family and was back for good. Another perfect piece fell into place. Another joy that forever warmed Leo's heart.

The pinnacle of happiness for Leo during that time came when she was finally able to fulfill a promise: for the first time ever, they all set foot inside an airplane and flew to an island to enjoy a well-deserved vacation. None of the members of the Peña family have forgotten how, step by step, they approached the white and red airplane of the most recognized commercial airline of the time. They will forever remember the tingling they felt in their stomachs when the large winged vehicle lifted its wheels off the ground, and then, looking through the windows, they saw cotton-like clouds decorating the blue sky... They were so close that they almost seemed touchable. Leo was in awe. Once again, she could prove to herself that this was the most appropriate way to live, in peace and with hard work.

As the days went by, one by one, they began to graduate from school. It was time to think about the universities they would attend. Everyone was looking to the future differently now. The past was buried and forgotten, and everyone's idea was always to find a way to help their mother, that woman who had been reborn by the anguish reflected in the eyes of her children, and who little by little, with much sacrifice, turned it into happiness.

Leo always thought, almost to the point of obsession, that her children should study. Even though she was a skilled and fierce woman, she couldn't imagine how far she could have gone if she had studied more than the few years she did as a child. But that was a thought only she had because everyone who knew her, including her children, could only feel admiration for such a strong and business-savvy woman. "And to think she barely knows how to sign a check," her children would say whenever someone praised their mother.

And it wasn't far from the truth; when going to the bank, Leo never went alone. She always went accompanied by one of her children to guide her in case she needed to read something. This made her feel embarrassed, but her children, as always, were her great team, her warriors... They never made fun of the situation, nor were they embarrassed by it. Leo was a born worker, and they learned about business and accounting just by watching how she handled things.

Eliseo began to save, and with Leo's help, he was able to purchase a newer car, which he would use to go to the university, located far from where they were living. Being a responsible young man, he organized his days in such a way that he had time to attend his classes, take his siblings wherever they needed to go, and help his mother to avoid using the crowded public transportation.

Life couldn't be more perfect. Daily challenges were managed calmly, as there was family support. Each and every member of the family were pillars that held up their own lives and those of others. Everyone relied on everyone else, and Leo, always at the forefront, commanded the ship she had set afloat and now kept above the waves of harmony with love, teachings, and hard work. Now, it was evident that together, they would all reach a safe harbor.

Chapter VII

How a journey through life can straighten its paths with inspiration and strength is what Leo demonstrated throughout her existence. The most tangible example is her children, who, despite the obstacles they encountered day by day, she managed to turn into successful and good individuals. With drive, hard work, concern, and love, she ensured that each one of them reached the pinnacle of their earthly existence.

Over time, Leo's eight children developed into triumphant individuals. For her, it was like a waking dream, which, thanks to her hard work, transformed into a tangible reality. Her desire was for them to study, and she achieved that; to become wholly productive individuals in their lives and society; to form stable families and continue to firmly anchor the legacy she left them on earth, despite the mistakes made along the way: a love for everything they do in life and that tireless capacity to recover and conquer with even more strength.

Alirio, her eldest son, always very intelligent and dedicated, passionate about reading and helping others, decided that his future lay in law. Thus, he chose to study Law, and eventually graduated as a lawyer from a renowned university.

Isaura's professional life developed in the classroom. Her love for teaching, for imparting knowledge, and for shaping people of excellence for the country and humanity led her to graduate as an educator. She pursued this career with passion for many years, teaching in high schools and even at universities.

Margarita devoted herself to the commendable task of building a home. She simply decided that her life was at home, and that her contribution to life would be to give love to all the members of her family. Much like her mother did with her and her siblings, she raised them to be well-rounded individuals for life.

As for Eliseo, Leo's guardian angel for many years, he leveraged his curiosity about how the world works and graduated as a metallurgical engineer.

Yolanda pursued the path of science and studied Chemistry and Biology. Arbello, who always showed a love for rural life, earned a degree in Agricultural Administration, a career that brought him much satisfaction throughout his life.

Asariel immersed himself in stacks of large paper sheets while studying Industrial Technical Drawing. Jesús, on the other hand, graduated from high school and, like his mother, engaged in the trade of various products that would benefit the local residents and provide income to support his family.

Despite their significant personal achievements, Leo never attended any of her children's graduations. "That's not for me," she would say every time one of them arrived with a formal invitation to attend the solemn ceremony. She believed it was each individual's responsibility to attend and saw the event as a mere formality. For her, the most important thing was that they graduated and developed their careers to establish stable and virtuous families.

Embracing her satisfaction, Leo continued to grow in life and business, and over the years, those who knew her, whether through business or personal relationships, began to call her "Doña Leo," two words that expressed respect, not so much for her age but for everything she had achieved in life and what she represented in the community of traders.

Always with the support of her children, Leo expanded the three-story buildings she had painstakingly constructed, block by block. They became increasingly spacious and comfortable. She also built a warehouse where she sold her products and those acquired from nearby markets. However, with an ever-present desire to grow even more, she was not content with this and saw another dream come true when she purchased a large estate on the Bogotá savanna, where she could brand her own cattle with her initials using a hot iron. Additionally, on the estate, she continued her poultry farming, which had always been her major business.

The family's finances not only improved but grew to levels that even Doña Leo herself could not have imagined. Yet, it was never enough, not only out of fear of falling into bankruptcy once again in her life but because her nature never allowed her to sit still. Doña Leo was in perpetual motion, always doing something, like the ant that tirelessly works for the benefit of her family nucleus. Despite being more than financially stable, she never stopped getting up before sunrise. By four in the morning, she was already up and about, knowing everything she would do throughout the day, beyond the time when the sun set behind the mountains. Going out into the street, trading, buying, selling, walking, immersing herself in the scents of the markets, navigating the aisles of stalls, greeting, sharpening her senses, seeking opportunities, and fiercely protecting and supporting her family – this was the day-to-day life of this great lady. "As long as my body allows it, one must work; money doesn't come on its own, it's out there, and you have to go and find it," she would repeat over and over, like the mantra that governed her entire life.

She knew that her work had brought her to where she was, that her effort had allowed her to once again take her children's hands and climb the mountain of success. However, she was also grateful for life. Both she and her children were always sure that an angel watched over them from somewhere in the universe. Despite everything they had experienced during the tough times and Doña Leo's missteps, nothing bad had ever happened to them, and they had always stayed on the path of righteous existence.

In the market, everyone recognized Doña Leo. When she made her way through stalls filled with merchandise, buyers, and sellers, the respect and admiration that everyone felt for her were palpable. Countless greetings, courtesies, and displays of affection filled her with immense satisfaction. This respect was not given freely; people admired her for how she had managed to bring up all her children. Even though they were now professionals with good economic standing, she continued to work day in and day out as if she had nothing or wanted to achieve something unattainable.

The years when Leo got into trouble with men were long gone. The times when her life revolved around a bottle of liquor accompanied by a bad character were buried. It could now be said, with all sincerity, that she was a new woman, devoted to her family, free from vices, and always willing to lend a hand to anyone in need. They say that anyone who visited her at home would be sure to find a good meal on her table; even in the market, many homeless people and individuals with serious economic and family limitations would approach her seeking help, and she would extend a helping hand.

Among many things, Doña Leo was also known for her fleet of trucks, a product of hard work. These vehicles could be seen daily on the streets of the markets, loaded with her chickens, which were selected for sale. "Get ready, here come Doña Leo's trucks loaded up," you would hear in the square as the large metal trucks appeared around the corner.

But not all the birds stayed there. Two of the large trucks were exclusively used to transport chickens to different parts of the country and deliver them to various restaurants and markets. Leo, without consciously intending to, became the largest wholesaler in the Bogotá central market.

Despite her success, none of her children went into the poultry business. Each one fully devoted themselves to their professional careers, which is what she preferred. She thought that it was a physically demanding job to which she was already accustomed, and that after making so much effort to ensure that they all succeeded and achieved stability and comfort, it was time for them to become independent and make their own living in their chosen fields, fully realizing themselves.

With the passage of years and the weight of age, Doña Leo's character hardened. Despite remaining a person with a big heart, any decision her children made in life had to undergo strict scrutiny by her before she would give her final approval or disapproval to their proposals.

As a natural law of life, the family grew little by little. Her children, all working and independent, began to form bonds with the people they had chosen to spend the autumn of their lives with, and these couples did not escape the watchful eye of Doña Leo, as they needed her approval to be welcomed into the family circle. She made it very clear, with her strong character, that she would never tolerate any mistreatment between her children and their partners. She always demanded respect and unity and became a protective and demanding mother, to the point that she didn't allow any of her children to drink or smoke in her presence because she knew the harm of those vices and wanted to keep them away from her children.

Although each of them managed to buy their own property in Bogotá to start their own families after getting married, they spent their vacations together as a family. They enjoyed beautiful moments traveling to the beaches of Santa Marta, Barranquilla, and Cartagena. They had the opportunity to visit Europe and the United States. What was amusing about these trips was that, even though they were already adults, Leo always protected them like children. Even on these trips, she would buy them curious gifts. It was clear that she always wanted to compensate for the difficult times they had experienced during their childhood, as a way to erase or make up for all the nightmares they had gone through a long time ago.

At this point, it could be said that Doña Leo had everything in life. But life rewarded her even more as her home gradually filled with the visits of her grandchildren.

By that time, Colombia was going through a critical and dangerous period. Every day, news of the armed conflict between the police and the military against the drug trafficker and leader of the Medellin Cartel, Pablo Escobar, filled the headlines. Leo watched on the news as kidnappings increased, how children were indoctrinated and trained to use them as sellers of the nefarious product. She was concerned that this organization of evil offered dreams of greatness and wealth to those who joined their ranks. She knew very well that her children were good people, and there was no problem on that front, but she was distressed by the possibility of something happening to them or her grandchildren going down the wrong path in the future, deceived by the false idea of an easy life filled with luxury. This led her to have even more control over her children's day-to-day lives. She asked them to inform her of their whereabouts and activities regularly, and if she considered a place unsafe, she made it clear with all the force of her imposing command voice. And for good reason, she had worked hard to raise her children, and she wasn't about to let "some scoundrel come and lead her family down a path of tragedy."

Thanks to the Almighty, none of that happened. Doña Leo's family continued on its natural course. Her name, teachings, life lessons, love, and many other things passed on successfully to her children and grandchildren.

Alirio had two children, one who followed in his footsteps and became a lawyer, and another who graduated from university as an economist. Isaura raised two doctors and an engineer. Margarita had three children, all of them engineers. Eliseo had four children, two daughters studying, one in the field of marketing and business, and the second in the field of social communication, and two self-employed entrepreneurs. Arbello had a son who became a journalist, a successful trader, and a very intelligent and curious daughter who became an expert in criminology. Asariel saw one of his sons become a journalist and another become a trader. Finally, Jesús, who shared his mother Leo's stories with his daughters, and they developed into expert traders in their own right.

A humorous family anecdote that was often talked about was when Alirio decided not to baptize his son. He believed that when his children grew up, they would decide for themselves which religion to follow. But Leo, once again demonstrating her strong character, decided not to allow her first grandson to go unbaptized. She called Eliseo to pick her up. When he arrived, she didn't mention her plan at all. Instead, she asked him to take her to buy a suit for a boy and then they went to Alirio's house to pick up the infant. Under the pretense of taking a short walk, they took the child directly to the church. Eliseo was astonished when Leo demanded that the priest baptize the child right at that moment. For those who later learned of this story, it became clear that Doña Leo never wasted time in her days, and she would always demonstrate her strong and decisive character when necessary, for she was a woman with a single-minded determination. She had very clear ideas and couldn't be persuaded otherwise.

Despite her strong character, her eight children dedicated their lives to her. They all knew very well that the foundation of their own families was the important influence of Leo in their lives and her invaluable legacy for the years to come. Without her, her efforts and teachings, they wouldn't be where they were. Despite the tough situations they had experienced in the past, such as abuse, abandonment, and poverty, they only had in mind to make her proud of everything they had achieved in life and to honor her as she deserved.

They feel pride in their mother, a deep admiration for the woman who, from nothing, from the ground up, took each of them by the hand and guided them to the pinnacle of success. No one can find the words to express the amazement and joy that she generates, that a virtually illiterate woman molded the clay of her children's lives one by one, the great potter, raising them all up healthily, with decent work, without harming anyone, without getting involved in illicit businesses, only through hard work and supporting each of their projects, always preventing them from making the same mistakes she made.

Her own children refer to her as "Leo, a police officer in the proper conduct of her children."

Chapter VIII

The inexorable passage of the years turned Doña Leo's hair silver-gray, and her strength began to wane in the natural spiral of life. Nevertheless, she continued her daily routine of work and looking after the well-being of her children and grandchildren. At sixty-five well-lived years, she began to work fewer hours a day. This was against the wishes of her children, who explained to her that she had no need to continue with her daily toil, as they, thanks to the Creator and their mother's teachings, could now support her and cover all her life's needs. They all thought that she had already done everything necessary to get ahead and that it was time to rest. But it was in vain. The Doña Leo that everyone knew would never allow others to support her, even if they were her own flesh and blood. Her strong character and attitude towards life never allowed her to stay in bed beyond five in the morning, even though sometimes her own body told her to take things slowly, and she understood it; she was no longer the same... It's okay, but still, she would not stop working.

Her children's eyes saw how Leo was gradually withering away. They knew that, as a law of life, flowers could not be alive forever. Conscious of their mother's autumn years, besides asking her to rest, they began an intense campaign to persuade Leo to attend medical check-ups that her age warranted, even though the response was always the same: "I'll go to the doctors when I have very strong pain... Otherwise... it's unnecessary."

But there are natural situations that even the strongest character cannot avoid. Doña Leo began to feel increasingly weakened. She was no longer the same. She felt like day by day, her strength was fading away, and even getting out of bed had become a daily challenge.

Eliseo couldn't stand by and do nothing while he witnessed his mother's daily struggle. Using all the powers of persuasion he had acquired over the years in his professional career, he convinced her to attend a medical appointment as soon as possible to determine the cause of her recent discomfort.

Doña Leo agreed. She underwent a series of tests that she found extremely bothersome and uncomfortable. She just wanted to return home as soon as possible. But deep down, she didn't want to worry Eliseo any further, and, deeper down, she knew that she was no longer the same, and all of this was for her own good.

Once all the initial tests were completed, and sitting face to face with the doctor, he explained very calmly but with the seriousness the case required that Doña Leo had severe blood pressure problems, high cholesterol, and the addition of diabetes.

The doctor took a moment alone with Eliseo to explain that his mother needed someone by her side to ensure she took all her medications exactly as prescribed. The doctor had immediately noticed Doña Leo's stubbornness and chose to discreetly offer this recommendation to Eliseo to avoid a resounding refusal from the patient.

Not more than a block had passed when Eliseo, who hadn't uttered a single word, heard his mother's voice, reminiscent of a military command:

"Don't you dare give orders to me. I know how to handle my affairs, and I know when to return to the clinic for my tests. I also know what I should eat and what I shouldn't."

Although he wanted to say a million words that crossed his mind at that moment, Eliseo remained silent throughout the journey back home.

Both he and his siblings knew it wouldn't be an easy task, as they were well aware of their mother's character. They all put in a lot of effort to make sure Leo followed what was agreed upon with the specialist, but in the end, everything always happened in her unique way.

It didn't take many months for another visit to the doctor, but this time it was an emergency: Doña Leo had suffered a major stroke. Everyone thought her end had come. Leo spent seven days in a coma. Seven long days that passed slowly, casting bitterness and worry on the faces of her children. Endless hours were spent by her side, not saying a word, only listening to the sound of the machines announcing the faint beating of Leo's heart. A steady but hopeful pulse... There was still life within that body.

One morning, on a fortunate day, Leo woke up. She barely recognized her children. Her gaze was fixed on the ceiling of an expensive and renowned clinic in Bogotá. She spent several weeks in the intensive care unit, surrounded by machines that monitored her existence in this earthly world.

She received rigorous treatment because the stroke had severely affected a large part of her brain, and the only option was to try to reduce the clots before subjecting her to a risky operation to improve her quality of life.

Leo spent more than two months bedridden. Over sixty days during which her children took turns to be by her side, constantly vigilant. Days when doctors expressed their surprise at Leo's determination to survive this episode, to make a full recovery, to return home, and continue with her daily activities.

The doctors managed to stabilize her and successfully perform the surgery, but her body was already very weakened. She was discharged from the hospital, allowed to go home, but despite the efforts of the medical team, Leo was extremely debilitated. The girl who had walked through the fields learning the trade from her father, the young woman who visited the markets daily, who moved with her children on foot, who worked with cattle and poultry, now had to remain in a wheelchair. She couldn't speak and could barely move. The Leo of constant motion was now a distant memory.

Anguish and depression began to create problems among Doña Leo's children. The distress of seeing their mother in this state clouded their minds and vision. Like Leo, they felt like they were no longer themselves, unable to think clearly. Eliseo, with the help of his siblings, paid the exorbitant medical bill left by the clinic. He did it with love because for him, always being the guardian angel, his mother's life and well-being were worth more than all the money, treasures, and castles in the world.

The siblings divided into two camps: those who argued that the best thing for Leo was for her to be in a nursing home, where she could receive around-the-clock care, allowing them to continue working as they had been; and those who, including Eliseo, believed that their mother didn't deserve to have such an ending, "abandoned in a place for the elderly," after everything she had fought for to raise them and see her children happy and united in life.

Until one day an agreement could be reached: Isaura would take her mother to her house to be with her family.

Everyone stayed in constant communication and remained alert to assist and attend to her sister at any sign or situation related to Leo.

All decisions made in these moments of life tend to be painful. They are mazes that close family members enter seeking the best way out. Once the agreement was reached on what would be the best way to provide peace and deserving care to Doña Leo, the question arose of what to do with her house, that large house she loved so much, that she bought with so much effort, that building where everyone lived at some point and later she saw its hallways and rooms filled with beloved grandchildren.

All subsequent expenses were covered by the properties, thereby covering Leo's monthly medical expenses without financially affecting any of her children, who, while they were stable, she would never have agreed to be a burden for them... In this way, everything became more bearable.

The Peña siblings began to navigate the situation as a great team, all for the benefit of their mother. Everything improved when each of them understood the suffering Leo was going through; that nothing they could be experiencing or feeling at that time could compare to what their mother held inside, seeing herself in such a state after having been such an active person and not being able to take care of herself. They realized that if the situation continued like this, it would end her sooner rather than later. The children had no choice but to continue with their lives. Some left Bogotá to pursue their respective careers.

In everyone's mind, there was always hope for Doña Leo's recovery. It wasn't just the typical thought of a child, a close family member, or a loved one; everyone's hope clung to the strength that Leo always showed throughout her life, a mental, spiritual, and physical force that always took her where she wanted to go, that infinite resilience. They hoped that at least she would speak, communicate with them, be able to say how she felt, recall and tell her grandchildren tales of past adventures; in short, that she would be at least a quarter of the Leo that everyone loved and admired.

But sadly, no, that long-awaited recovery did not come. With each passing day, it worsened. Leo's vital light was fading. The flower of her existence withered.

On a particularly bad day, her breathing started to fail. In Leo's eyes, one could see the desperation of intermittent suffocation. Everything was immediately arranged for her to start medical therapy to improve her clinical condition. The goal was to keep her as comfortable as possible; she didn't deserve any kind of suffering... Eleven years had passed since the downward spiral of Doña Leo began, and sadly, there wasn't much left to do. Seeing her increasingly destabilized, the decision was made to take her to the specialized clinic in Bogotá.

On a cold, rainy morning, January 16, 2003, Doña Leo's soul departed from the earthly plane. A last and brief sigh marked the end of this great woman. Like a fast-forwarded movie, Leo's life played in the minds of her children: her teachings, her love, her passion for work, her successes and mistakes. She was seventy-eight when her body decided to stop fighting.

An intense, powerful, torn battle that anyone else would have lost a long time ago, but not Leo, not that being full of strength and vitality. How immense was the void Doña Leo left that morning, how vast the world became without her.

From a block away, one could smell the scent of flowers emanating from the viewing room where Leo's coffin was placed, and yet, more flower arrangements kept arriving, sent by various people as a sign of respect and admiration for this woman. All her children were present at the funeral. Everyone who loved and knew her. The service lasted two days, and it seemed like it would be short given the number of people who came to show their respects. Many who had worked with her attended. Those passing by the street in front were puzzled to see such a gathering and, curious about the event, approached just to ask which public figure had passed away to cause such a stir.

The burial was no different; the entire neighborhood attended the cemetery. Faces filled with tears as the coffin containing Leo's body began to descend to its final resting place. Tears that lingered as the raindrops that fell the morning Doña Leo left the earth. Among those present, a familiar face that hadn't been seen in a long time was spotted: Miguelito was there, forgiving the past, showing the deepest pain for the loss of who was a mother to him.

Now, under a gravestone inscribed with Leovigilda Peña Monroy, rests the body of Doña Leo. Only her body is there; her soul remains alive in the daily lives of those who remember her with love and respect. This wonderful human being left a mark on all who knew her during her time on earth, and as the years pass, her distinguished family legacy will be perpetuated: tenacity, perseverance, and unending love for her own.